ROOTS AND PILLARS
OF FAITH

A Spiritual Classic on the Potency and Efficacy of Faith

MACHI MIKE OKENWA

CONTENTS

Acknowledgments

Foreword vii

Preface ix

Introduction xiii

.... xvii

PART I

THE CONCEPT OF FAITH

1. The Description And Definition of Faith

2. The Availability of Faith 3

3. The Two Kinds of Faith 9

4. The Source of Faith 15

5. Faith Is Warfare 25

6. Faith Is The Lifestyle of the Righteous 31

7. Faith Is A Weapon 39

8. The Legality of Faith 47

9. The Relationship Between Faith, Belief, and Receive ... 59

10. Grace and Faith 63

.... 67

PART II

ROOTS AND PILLARS OF FAITH

Background Information

11. The Almighty God - The Root and Pillar of Our Faith ... 77

12. Christ - The Root and Pillar of Our Faith 79

13. The Holy Spirit - The Root and Pillar of Our Faith ... 85

14. The Word of God - The Root and Pillar of Our Faith ... 91

15. Love - The Root and Pillar of Our Faith 99

16. Patience - Pillar of Our Faith 103

17. Prayer - Pillar of Our Faith 115

18. Confession (Declaration) - Pillar of Our Faith . 125

19. Sound Mind - Pillar of Our Faith 129

.... 139

20. Steadfastness - Pillar of Our Faith   157
21. Boldness - Pillar of Faith   165
22. Persuasion - Pillar of Faith   171
23. Imagination - Pillar of Faith   181
24. Thanksgiving - A Pillar of Faith   189
25. Grace - The Super Pillar of Faith   195
    Let Us Know...   201

DEDICATION

This piece of anointed literature is dedicated to the Almighty God, the Father of our Lord Jesus Christ who saved me and called me with a holy calling, not according to my works, but according to His own purpose and grace, which was given to me in Christ Jesus before the world began (II Timothy 1:9).

And to the human inhabitants of the planet Earth, who seriously need this equipment of the supernatural weapon of faith to know God (through His son Jesus Christ) and to dominate this fallen world of unprecedented wickedness and ungodliness; I dedicate this book.

ACKNOWLEDGMENTS

The first fruits of my gratitude will always go to my unrivaled teacher (the Mighty Holy Spirit). As long as I am prepared to listen, He is always available to educate me and reveal to me the mysteries of the Word and the Kingdom of God. Thank you precious Holy Spirit.

I will profoundly acknowledge my precious, powerful, anointed, and victorious wife, mother, and friend - Mama Ruth Okenwa - and all the members of my family for their support of sweet smelling savor.

My sincere gratitude is to Apostle Udechi Chukwu of Full-Life Christian Assembly, Inc. in Bronx, New York, and his blessed congregation. God used this supernatural fellowship of brethren to break the power of procrastination that hindered this divine assignment for years. Sometimes our faith needs a divine push, while at the same time it is complemented by others as one will chase a thousand but two chase ten thousand.

Thank you Pastor Taiwo Ayeni for your editorial excellence, your strategy of detailed perusal is without rival.

Kristina M. Rogers of Letters and Marques has always done a great and excellent job working on the transcription of our tapes and also typing them out as manuscripts. Thank you, Kristy.

I lack words to express my gratitude to a dynamic man of God, Brother Kris Ernest Enemo, whom God has appointed as an indispensable supportive pillar in all we do in the ministry of which this book is a tiny portion. I wish to also acknowledge members of his household who participated in the typing of the manuscripts.

The anointed members of New Creation Freedom Fellowship: especially Elder Uzo and Sister Edna, Pastor Chris, the Okpulors, Pastor Betty Ogaye, Evangelist Eunice, and many others deserve my acknowledgement for their endless ministerial supports.

I declare a posthumous thank you to my late father, Michael Okenwa, and mother Rhoda Okenwa. When I was five years old and throughout my elementary school career he woke me up by 4.00 am (Monday through Friday) and compelled me to study and memorize materials before going to school, while my late mother prayed for me before and after bedtime daily.

Finally, I also thank and acknowledge the many pastors, writers, and members of the body of Christ who in many ways contributed to my knowledge, spiritual growth and maturity.

FOREWORD

Small things, they say, come in small packages. Right? While this may be true in a lot of situations, in this circumstance it is not so, because this book, in your hands now, though small in size, vehemently defies this adage.

Roots and Pillars of Faith provides the core solution for someone with the desire to excel and come to the sound knowledge of who God has purposed him to be. It unveils the clear path towards practical Christianity.

This book, as it were, leads you from the basics and fundamentals of faith, to the heights of the realization of your authority as a divine child of the Most High God. It is important that you know that the whole machinery of the universe is maintained by faith. Without faith, it is impossible to please Him (Hebrews 11:6). And as we see confirmed in Matthew 9:29 "***According to your faith be it*** (done) ***unto you.***"This means "it will be done unto you". It is not you who is going to do it; it will be done unto you, by a force and power greater than you: the power of the Holy Spirit. Again, we read, ".....*If ye have faith as a grain of mustard seed, ye shall say unto this mountain, Remove hence to yonder place; and it shall remove; and nothing shall be impossible unto you.*" (Matthew 17:20).

It is all about faith, and without faith nothing can be done unto you. Faith without doubt, is a supernatural key to victorious human existence.

How does one go about acquiring this very vital and indispensable commodity called "faith?" The answer is simple, even simpler than the question - keep reading. Yes, just keep exploring this book; not just reading, but keep reading with meditation and cognition. As you continue to read, you will be built up in your most holy faith (Jude: 20). The Spirit in you will rise and so also shall your faith. No other action is required.

Are you not glad? Pastor Mike, uses his vast knowledge of the WORD to not only reaffirm his statements, but also to encourage the reader to realize that God is the same yesterday, today and forever (Hebrews 13:8). What God has done for one, He can and will do for the other - "God is no respecter of persons," (Acts10:34); and He has no favorites. However, you must know and be conscious of this fact. You must also be able to put what you are reading into action. Faith without works is dead, (James 2:26).

Faith is believing and acting on the Word of God, irrespective of the challenging physical evidence. The only way for you to enjoy and benefit from the food menu in a fine restaurant, is actually to order from the menu and eat! In the same manner you must put the knowledge from this book into practice. Taste, see, and know that the Lord is good.

Roots & Pillars of Faith is not just another book hot off the press; it is a book to be read, re-read and passed on. Therefore, get copies for yourself, friends and neighbors and inspire open doors of divine exploits in your life and theirs.

Kris Ernest Enemo
May 26th, 2018

PREFACE

Moment by moment, God impresses in my heart to continuously write about the purpose of enforcing, advancing, and enlarging His Kingdom on the planet Earth. For this reason I believe, He will always flood my spiritual eyes of understanding with unimaginable revelation, deep spiritual eyesight and insights. The confirmation of this fact also came through many prophecies.

Unfortunately, I adopted a fruitless strategy of writing notes without converting them into books. As a result, I ended up with piles of notebooks and papers full of biblical information that I cannot peruse and compile into any book. Miraculously, the invitation of my honorable pastor friend and brother in Christ (Apostle Udechi Chukwu, of Full-Life Christian Assembly, Inc. in Bronx, New York) broke the back of this error when I taught on faith in his prayer line fellowship.

I said "miraculously" because the invitation, the teaching, and the congregation became the catalyst that inspired and energized me to pursue the production of this book as one of a series on faith.

Prior to the reminder received as per my divine calling, which is writing for the Kingdom, my Christian life experience was defined by miraculous manifestations, borne out of practical application of biblical faith. Unfortunately, I had no space to include those testimonies (except one) in this book. Subsequent books on faith will definitely carry them because they are significant, uplifting, and full of inspirations.

Biblical faith (faith which the object is God and His infallible word of truth) is a supernatural force that is failure proof. This is true because the word of God is defined as incorruptible seed in I Peter 1:23. People fail in their knowledge and application of human faith, but not in the knowledge and application of the faith of the operation of God (Colossians 2:12). The operation of God's faith cannot fail. It's supernatural by nature and will be fully discussed in this book.

"If we believe not, yet he (God) abideth faithful: he cannot deny himself." (II Timothy 2:13 KJV)

"Faithful is he that calleth you, who also will do it." (I Thessalonians 5:24 KJV)

Prayerfully prepare yourself to be educated, trained, and equipped as a warrior of Zion ready to operate in the realm and battlefield of faith. As you fight the good fight of faith (I Timothy 6:12) and contend for the faith which was once delivered unto the saints (Jude 1:3), I declare to you that victory and triumph would be your reward (I John 5:4; I Corinthians 15:57; II Corinthians 2:14). The abundance of grace and the gift of righteousness you received at the point of regeneration is at work in your life; empowering and energizing you to rule in the midst of relentless unfavorable and challenging circumstances of the fallen planet earth (Romans 5:17).

The exceedingly great and mighty resurrection power of Christ is engaged in your circumstances and situations for your good if you master the art of the good fight of faith. (Ephesians 1:19; Galatians 2:20; Colossians 1:29; Philippians 2:13).

Finally, the incorruptible seed, powerful, and living Word of God is working mightily on your behalf and will prevail in every department of your life; according to the order of the city of Ephesus (Hebrews 4:12; I Thessalonians 2:13; Acts 19:20).

Remain strong in the Lord and in His mighty power in Jesus name (Ephesians 6:10).

Pastor Machi Mike Okenwa

INTRODUCTION

"Now faith is the substance of things hoped for, the evidence of things not seen" (Hebrews 11:1 KJV)

Clearly we see that faith is the spiritual substance (relevant Word of God because faith comes by hearing the Word of God - Romans 10:17) of our hopeful expectation. It's also the spiritual evidence (proof - relevant Word of God) of our unseen realities. If you can see it, you don't need faith because faith deals with the invisible only. It calls the things that be not as though they were (Romans 4:17). Whatever you cannot see (but desired), if you tenaciously engage the spiritual laws of faith with boldness and confidence; as unveiled in this book, you can provoke the manifestation of that expectation. That is what faith is all about.

This is the first book in our faith collection series on the concept and application of faith. If the spiritual rules of the engagement of faith are not religiously applied, the efficacy and inevitability of faith will not be manifested. The Bible confirms the dynamic creative capacity of the faith of the operation of God (Colossians 2:12), which is the same as the faith of Jesus Christ (Galatians 2:16, 20). This faith is responsible for the existence of the universe (with all its faculties and complexities) and humanity.

Whatever you cannot see (but desired), if you tenaciously engage the spiritual laws of faith - as unveiled in this book, with boldness and confidence - you can provoke the manifestation of that expectation.

Even God (the Creator—Isaiah 40:28-31) is a God of faith (Colossians 2:12). He calls those things that be not as though they were (Romans 4:17). As a result, without faith, man who is the heartbeat of God will forever be lost and spiritually separated from Him. For without faith it is impossible to please (or relate) to God (Hebrews 11:6).

Faith is a supernatural agency with numerous characteristics. However, the prominent elements that granted faith the nature of dynamism, creativity, and ruler-ship are that:

i) Faith is of God (Ephesians 2:8-9; Romans 10:17;

Romans 4:17).

ii) Faith is a law (Romans 3:27).

iii) Faith is a spirit (II Corinthians 4:13).

iv) Faith is a weapon (I John 5:4; Ephesians 6:16).

V) Faith is the most potent force in the universe (Matthew17:20).

Indeed faith is a container of abundance of dominion.

".....If ye have faith as a grain of mustard seed, ye shall say unto this mountain, Remove hence to yonder place; and it shall remove; and nothing shall be impossible unto you." (Matthew 17:20 KJV)

Faith is one face of the spiritual currency for supernatural transactions in the Kingdom of God; Grace is the other face. As promised earlier, please find hereunder my testimony:

One faithful occasion I took a test on a job interview. I was negatively informed that I failed the test, but they promised to allow me do a retake of the test on a different date. However, I told them that I did not fail any test because I have the mind of Christ as it is written in 1 Corinthians 2:16. I blamed their iPad and devil for lying against me. They laughed at me hilariously as I insisted that I will not retake the test. Three days later the job was offered to me and this is my fifth year at that job. Glory be to God! Faith works only if you patiently work it without doubting.

No doubt, the grace of God freely provides all our needs in the Kingdom of God (Romans 4:16; Romans 8:32; II Corinthians 4:15; I Corinthians 3:20-23; I Corinthians 2:12). But faith enables the children of the Kingdom to freely take hold of or appropriate them.

"And as ye go, preach, saying, The kingdom of heaven is at hand.

Heal the sick, cleanse the lepers, raise the dead, cast out devils: freely ye have received, freely give." (Matthew 10:7-8)

Note: *"Freely you have received, freely you give."* The word "freely" is synonymous with grace in the Bible. Grace is the supernatural foundation of the blessings and dominion capacity God credited to the accounts of all believers; as a by-product of the finished work of the cross by Jesus Christ.

"For if by one man's offence death reigned by one; much more they which receive abundance of grace and of the gift of righteousness shall reign in life by one, Jesus Christ." (Romans 5:17 KJV)

Our ability to rule, control and dominate life on earth, as new creations in Christ, is a product of our gift of grace and righteousness. Like faith, righteousness is another companion of grace.

Faith is one face of the spiritual currency for supernatural transactions in the Kingdom of God; Grace is the other face.

The unshakable and unmovable kingdom we have received (Hebrews 12:28) is loaded with grace, gift of righteousness, rulership capacity and ability, dominion, faith and so much more. Of course, the fullness of the grace and the truth of God is manifest in Christ Jesus (John 1:14). Christ is also the grace of God that brought salvation to all men:

"Teaching us that denying ungodliness and worldly lusts, we should live soberly, righteously, and godly, in this present world.

Looking for that blessed hope, and the glorious appearing of the Great God and our savior Jesus Christ.

Who gave himself for us, that he might redeem us from all iniquity, and purify unto himself, a peculiar people, zealous of good work." (Titus 2:11-14 KJV)

Christ is the grace of God, the originator and finisher of our faith (Hebrews 12:3).

Having thrown much light on both sides (grace and faith) of the supernatural currency of the Kingdom of God, justice must be done to the "roots and pillars" of faith. The knowledge of roots and pillars of faith, as unveiled in this book will facilitate the practical effectiveness and productivity of any life dedicated to the faith of God and His son Jesus Christ (Colossians 2:12; Galatians 2:16, 20).

The abundance of grace and the gift of righteousness you received at the point of regeneration is at work in your life ; empowering and energizing you to rule in the midst of relentless unfavorable and challenging circumstances of the fallen planet earth.

Therefore, prepare yourself prayerfully as you study to show yourself approved unto God (11 Timothy 2:15a). Also, as you function in the realm of faith, do not forget "that the communication (practice) of thy faith may become effectual (productive) by the acknowledgment of every good thing which is in you in Christ Jesus - the root and pillar of your faith" (Philemon 1:6). Because without faith it is impossible to please Him. And, not only that, without faith, it's impossible to see and enter into His Kingdom and enjoy the everlasting life of God.

One might ask: what capacity of importance can be ascribed to the supernatural dynamics of faith in human affairs? Well, natural faith has tremendously contributed to the development and destruction of humanity. By faith, man manufactured commercial, private and military (fighter and bomber) aircrafts. However, God's kind of faith gloriously located the fallen and lost humanity, redeemed man from the bondage and penalty of sin, from the captivity of Satan and reconciled him with his creator and source of his life; with the everlasting gift of eternal life as recorded in the scriptures:

"For God so loved the world, that he gave his only begotten Son, that whosoever believeth (has faith) in him should not perish, but have everlasting life." (John 3:16 KJV) .

Everlasting life (the nature of God) is the product of faith in Jesus Christ, the Son of God.

PART I
THE CONCEPT OF FAITH

CHAPTER 1
THE DESCRIPTION AND DEFINITION OF FAITH

"**W**e *having the same <u>spirit of faith,</u> according as it is written, I believed, and therefore <u>have I spoken;</u> we also believe, and therefore <u>speak</u>.*" (II Corinthians 4:13 KJV)

"*And Jesus said unto them, Because of your unbelief (lack of faith): for verily I say unto you, If ye have <u>faith as a grain of mustard seed</u>, ye shall say unto this mountain, Remove hence to yonder place; <u>and it shall remove;</u> and <u>nothing shall be impossible</u> unto you.*" (Matthew 17:20 KJV)

So many lessons can be extracted from the passages of scriptures above and these are:

1. Faith is not an ordinary phenomenon, but a supernatural force with the capacity to do the miraculous. So, if you desire signs and wonders, faith is at your disposal to satisfy your thirst because faith is a spirit.
2. Faith is voice activated. I once heard a preacher say, "You

cannot face your Goliath (giant or challenges) with your mouth closed." A functional productive faith places a demand on your mouth and voice. Speak to the mountain (Mark 11:23). No voice, no productive faith!

3. Faith possesses the characteristics of a seed, and we all know that the nature of a seed is beyond human comprehension. No one can accurately predict whether a seed will germinate or not and how long it will take to germinate and how it does germinate. Even science does not have authentic and accurate explanation of the transformation that occurs in a seed planted. Imagine the fact that a seed has to die and experience resurrection from death before it springs out of the ground. Sometimes you notice a tiny plant bursting through a concrete slab with a flourishing life. This is difficult to either explain or comprehend. In a nutshell, like a seed, faith is miraculous by nature.

4. *"Ye shall say unto this mountain, Remove hence to yonder place, and it shall remove."* In other words, faith has unlimited capacity of dominance. It has authoritative and ruler-ship ability.

5. *"And nothing shall be impossible unto you."* Faith possesses the ability or capacity to overcome impossibility and render it powerless. It breaks the monstrous power of impossibility. *"If thou canst believe, all things are possible to him that believeth."* (Mark 9:23).

"Through faith also Sara herself received strength to conceive seed, and was delivered of a child when she was past age, because she judged him faithful who had promised.

"By faith the walls of Jericho fell down, after they were compassed about seven days."
"Women received their dead raised to life again......." (Hebrews 11:11, 30, 35a KJV)

Without exaggeration, the potency of faith is inexhaustible; (and bearing this in mind, we shall deal with more of them in other books in our faith collection series.)

So, if you desire signs and wonders, faith is at your disposal to satisfy your thirst because faith is a spirit.

Definition of Faith:

"Now faith is the substance of things hoped for, the evidence of things not seen." (Hebrews 11:1 KJV).

Many are frustrated in their practice of faith because they fail to recognize that faith is a present moment activity unlike hope which is futuristic in nature. For instance, there is no faith in saying that, "God is going to heal me." That is a no, no!

God is "going to" heal me is in the future - that basically is hope. Faith is a present issue phenomenon ("Now Faith is").

According to the Bible, faith is a substance. What does that mean?

This statement is saying that faith is not the reality of your expectation, but it gives substance to it. For example, if you're expecting healing in your body, faith is not the healing; but faith is a major substance (among others like "action" and "speaking") that will enable the realization of your healing. This explains what the Bible meant when it says: ".....*so faith without works is dead also*" (James 2:26). Faith as a substance, when in combination with other substances; gives birth to our expectation.

Faith is not an ordinary phenomenon, but a supernatural force with the capacity to do the miraculous.

In the natural, any attempt to produce cake will require substances like flour, sugar, egg, water, heat, etc. This procedure is applicable to faith. Faith (a substance according to scriptures), requires a combination of other substances like the word of God, heart, belief, speaking and patience; among many others.

If the foundation and object of your faith is God (the Father of our Lord Jesus Christ), then the substance of your faith is the word of God. The word of God (the Holy Scripture) definitely will give substance to the manifestation of your expectation.

Additionally, according to Hebrews 11:1, faith is evidence (proof). For instance; the title deed of my house or the title documents of my car are legally acceptable documentation of my ownership. These documents are so powerfully authentic that they can stand as acceptable collateral financial documents. Indeed, they are unquestionable evidence of ownership in any civilized economy.

It's important that we continue to emphasize the fact that faith is not your reality (expectation); but the evidence (proof) of your expectation (reality). Also, the challenge or your experience is not your reality. Again, if the object of your faith is God, then the evidence (proof) of your healing (expectation) is the corresponding healing Word of God. This is your reality (the corresponding promises of God). Thinking otherwise is the very mistake that places so many in the failure-realm of faith. For instance:

"When the even was come, they brought unto him (Christ) many that were possessed with devils: and he cast out the spirits with his word, and healed all that were sick;" (Matthew 8:16 KJV)

Jesus used the word of God to accomplish healing and deliverance.

"He sent his word, and healed them, and delivered them from their destructions." (Psalm 107:20 KJV)

So God also uses His word of faith to heal and to deliver. As a child of God (born of God - John 1:13), whose object of faith is God, the evidence (proof) of your healing and deliverance from evil spirits or addictions, etc. is the infallible word of God (also called the word of faith - Romans 10:8).

When some Christians declare that they believe God is going to heal them, ask them to show you their substance and evidence. You will be surprised to notice that they don't have any. The implication is that they are practicing mental-sense knowledge (human) faith as against revelatory knowledge faith of God, which is based on the word of God - faith comes by hearing the word of God (Romans 10:17). Mental or sense knowledge faith is a product of the senses and it is unreliable. This kind of faith is called human faith.

In another parlance, faith is the supernatural substance of our invisible expectation (hope); and the spiritual evidence (proof) of our unseen realities. When faith is righteously and judiciously applied, invisible expectations and unseen realities have no choice but to assume the status of physical manifestation.

A functional productive faith places a demand on your mouth and voice. Speak to the mountain (Mark 11:23). No voice, no productive faith!.

CHAPTER 2
THE AVAILABILITY OF FAITH

Many (Christians and non-Christians) complain that they don't have faith. But is that true? One day I had a pilot with me in my car, and as we were discussing my books on faith, he complained to me that one of his life challenges is lack of faith. I responded, "How can that be?" Moreover, I reminded him that he flies private jets which are most unstable in the air and prone to accidents when compared with big aircrafts. He confessed to me that small aircrafts are greatly challenged by elements of weather and air resistance. And those are the types he flies all the time.

Then I responded, "Do you know what you just told me? That one needs a tremendous amount of faith to fly small aircrafts. Moreover, I have come across people who do not travel by air because of fear. Also, we have now travelled over ten miles with me driving and you sitting comfortably, talking and enjoying the ride without fear. Why? It's because you have faith in my driving skills and in the manufacturer of the automobile. The same notion applies to you concerning your profession and the people you fly in your aircraft."

With humility, the issue and challenge is not the absence of faith but lack of knowledge and application of faith. Many people have no idea that they possess all the faith required to move any mountain in their lives. And some, who do know, lack the knowledge of how to release (use) their faith or put their faith to work.

As a child of God (born of God - John 1:13), whose object of faith is God, the evidence (proof) of your healing and deliverance from evil spirits or addictions, etc. is the infallible word of God (also called the word of faith - Romans 10:8).

Genesis 1:26 reveals the supernatural and natural authoritative dominion God granted humanity over the universe. But Genesis 1:28 even climaxed the mandate.

"And God blessed them, and God said unto them, Be fruitful, and multiply, and replenish the earth, and subdue it: and have dominion over the fish of the sea, and over the fowl of the air, and over every living thing that moveth upon the earth."

Tremendous proven evidences abound to show that man conquered the universe - he can fly the airplane as birds naturally fly. He can sail the ship afloat, and submerge the submarines just as fish naturally do. Man crafts pieces of iron to talk just as man can talk. He conquered the natural law of gravity, the natural law of float, space, land, and sea. How about his prowess in communication? How on earth is he able to accomplish all the uncountable, unimaginable, and over-whelming scientific, technological, medical, and social exploits? The answer is faith. It's written:

"For I say, Through the grace given unto me, to <u>every man</u> that is among you, not to think of himself more highly than he ought to think; but to think soberly, according as <u>God</u> hath dealt to every man the measure of faith." (Romans 12:3 KJV)

Every man was born into the Planet Earth with the measure of faith. Otherwise, how do you account for the fact that one can drive through a green traffic light without faith (trusting and believing) that the opposing traffic will stop at the red light signal? I tell you what, - we sit on a chair because we believe that it will sustain our weight. If we have any information contrary to the stability of the chair we'll decline to sit on it. We accept medication from the doctors and pharmacists believing they are the right ones. We accept and eat food from restaurants believing they are not poisonous. We jump into elevators believing we will not get stuck. Every positive action of man is an act of faith. How about stocks, security, and fixed assets investments?

Above are all actions of faith which sometimes hand us packages of failure and disappointment. These packages are not necessarily the products of our action of faith but of our object of faith. What is the object of your faith? Man's action of faith will succeed or fail if the object of faith is based on anything (like human resources and ability) other than God and in His word.

Additionally, every believer in Christ has received the following:

(1) The gift of faith:

"For by grace are ye saved through faith: and that not of yourselves: it is the gift of God" (Ephesians2:8). This signifies that our salvation is the product of the gift of grace and faith we received from God.

(2) We also received the spirit of faith as recorded in the following scriptures:

"We having the same spirit of faith, according as it is written; I believed and therefore have I spoken: we also believe, and therefore speak."(11Corinthians4:13).

(3) *"Like Precious Faith"*, is another package of faith that came with our salvation experience (11Peter1:1).

"Simon Peter; a servant and apostle of Jesus Christ, to them that have obtained like precious faith with us through the righteousness of God and our Saviour Jesus Christ".

(4) *"But what saith it? The word is nigh thee, even in thy mouth, and in thy heart: that is the word of faith, which we preach"* (Romans10:8). Again here, the Bible informs us that every believer in Christ possesses the word of faith in his mouth and in his heart. Evidently, our salvation experience came with inexhaustible gift of portfolio of faith.

In another parlance, faith is the supernatural substance of our invisible expectation (hope); and the spiritual evidence (proof) of our unseen realities.

This is included in the unsearchable riches of Christ. Again, the challenge is not the issue of absence of faith. Indeed, we have abundance of faith. The challenge is always: ignorance of our possession and application. This takes us to the next level of our discussion, which is the two kinds of faith.

CHAPTER 3
THE TWO KINDS OF FAITH

There are so many ways to classify faith. To me, the most fundamental, practical, and beneficial classification of faith is the one of two dimensions: human faith and the faith of God. Knowledge of these two kinds of faith is of paramount importance because it is the major factor responsible for the unproductive faith life of many. You might be surprised to note that majority of humanity practice human kind of faith instead of God's kind of faith.

Human Faith (Man's Kind of Faith):

Although God gave man the gift of the measure of faith, yet if man practices this faith independent of God and His word, the faith in question becomes the faith of man. It is also called the human faith or man's kind of faith. The object of the human faith is the senses. That's why it is sometimes called sense knowledge faith. The corresponding action of this kind of faith is based on the natural five senses (physical evidence of what we can see, smell, taste, hear, and feel or touch). This faith is subject to success as well as failure.

The Case of Thomas Didymus:

"But Thomas, one of the twelve, called Didymus, was not with them when Jesus came.

The other disciples therefore said unto him, we have seen the Lord. But he said unto them, Except I shall see in his hands the print of the nails, and put my finger into the print of the nails, and trust my hand into his side, I will not believe." (John 20:24-25 KJV)

Here, Thomas instead of believing the information given to him by his colleagues about the resurrection of Jesus, chose to rely on the physical evidence of his senses. This attitude or action typically describes the human faith or better called sense knowledge faith, that is operated according to the senses.

When faith is righteously and judiciously applied, invisible expectations and unseen realities have no choice but to assume the status of physical manifestation.

The problem with this kind of faith is that it's limited to the senses, and therefore unreliable and unproductive. Drivers sometimes run red lights at traffic junctions. Planes sometimes crash. Elevators sometimes get stuck. All these happen irrespective of trust and faith on the drivers, pilots, and manufacturers. That is the nature of human faith. Human faith is not perfect!

Thomas relied on his senses to convince himself about the reality of the resurrection of Jesus. When he eventually saw Jesus, he cried out, "*.....My Lord and my God. Jesus saith unto him, Thomas, because thou hast seen me, thou has believed: blessed are they that have not seen, and yet have believed.*" (John 20:28-29). Wow! Those who ignore faith and those who practice human faith are not blessed. Only those who practice faith based on God's word are blessed.

At one time, Apostle Peter was awaiting execution in prison. Then, the disciples gathered, locked up themselves and prayed; God executed a miraculous release of Peter by the hand of a powerful ministering Angel. But when Peter knocked at the door where the disciples gathered, they all responded with sense knowledge faith with the exception of Rhoda-an eye witness. This event was recorded as follows:

"And as Peter knocked at the door of the gate, a damsel came to hearken, named Rhoda. And when she knew Peter's voice, she opened not the gate for gladness, but ran in, and told how Peter stood before the gate. And they said unto her, thou at mad. But she constantly affirmed that it was even so. Then said they, it is his angel. But Peter continued knocking: and when they had opened the door, and saw him, they were astonished."(Acts12:13-16).

Here, the disciples engaged God in prayer for Peter's freedom; using human (sense knowledge) faith. Like Thomas, they refused to believe that their prayers have been answered until they saw Peter. Any application of faith with the senses as object of belief is nothing but human faith (the faith of a man) and it is subject to disappointment: with the exception of God's sovereign divine intervention.

The Faith of God (God's Kind of Faith):

God's kind of faith is listed in many places in the New Testament.

"Buried with him in baptism, wherein also ye are risen with him through the faith of the operation of God, who hath raised him from the dead." (Colossians 2:12 KJV)

This scripture teaches that it was the faith of God that raised Christ from the dead, together with all the believers who; in the realm of the spirit, went to the cross with Him. God's kind of faith is also called the faith of Christ.

"Knowing that a man is not justified by the works of the Law, but by the <u>faith of Jesus Christ</u>, even we have believed in Jesus Christ, that we might be justified by <u>the faith of Christ</u>, and not by the works of the law: for by the works of the law shall no flesh be justified." (Galatians 2:16 KJV)

Our salvation and justification (righteousness) are the products of God's kind of faith or the faith of Jesus Christ. The object of this faith is God and His word of faith (Romans 10:8). This faith trusts in God and acts on the Word of God independent of the senses and unfavorable hostile physical evidence. This supernatural faith calls the things that be not as though they were (Romans4:17). Jesus declared:

"Thomas, because thou hast seen me, thou hast believed; blessed are they that have not seen, and yet have believed." (John20:29).

"Therefore I say unto you, what things soever ye desire, when ye pray, believe that ye receive them, and ye shall have them." (Mark11:24).

God's kind of faith, believes, receives; independent of physical evidence or manifestation.

"For we walk by faith (God's kind of faith), *not by sight (the senses)."* (II Corinthians 5:7 KJV)

God's kind of faith not only laughs at impossibilities, it breaks its powers, thus:

"Jesus said unto him, If thou canst believe (corresponding action of faith), *all things are possible to him that believeth* (in God)." (Mark 9:23 KJV)

If you desire to deal victoriously with impossibilities, what you need is the faith of God.

"For with God nothing shall be impossible." (Luke 1:37 KJV). Also, *"If thou canst believe, all things are possible to him that believeth."* (Mark9:23)

God's kind of faith is dependent upon God and His word. It is insensitive to the senses and physical evidence. I had one man of God say, "I'm not moved by what I see, but I'm moved by what I believe."

Many people have no idea that they possess all the faith required to move any mountain in their lives. And some, who do know, lack the knowledge of how to release (use) their faith or put their faith to work.

The Case of Abraham:
"Now, Sarai, Abram's wife bare him no children: and she had an handmaid, an Egyptian, whose name was Hagar.

And Sarai said unto Abram, Behold now, the Lord hath restrained me from bearing: I pray thee, go in unto my maid; it may be that I may obtain children by her. And Abram harkened to the voice of Sarai." (Genesis 16:1-2 KJV)

So when Abram and Sarai in one accord considered the unfavorable physical condition of Sarai and acted upon their sense knowledge, Ishmael was produced instead of God's ordained Isaac. Humanity cannot deny the disastrous consequences (among them-terrorism) of this simple act of human faith by Abram and Sarai.

Nevertheless, a dramatic change of out- pouring of the blessings of God occurred when Abraham and his wife grew in their faith lifestyle and switched to God's kind of faith. Their action was not only dramatic and productive; it also constitutes one of the highest lessons on faith as recorded in the Bible. Apostle Paul wrote: Abraham;

"Who against hope believed in hope, that he might become the father of many nations; according to that which was spoken, So shall thy seed be.

And being not weak in faith, he considered not his own body now dead, when he was about an hundred years old, neither yet the deadness of Sarah's womb.

He staggered not at the promise of God through unbelief; but was strong in faith, giving glory to God.

And being fully persuaded that what he (God) *had promised* (the word of God), *he was able also to perform."* (Romans 4:18-21 KJV)

At this point in time, Abraham completely rejected sense

knowledge human faith and embraced God's kind of faith which acts on the word of God, regardless of the aggressive and unfavorable physical evidence of old age. As a result, Isaac was begotten - the promised one. Isaac, like all believers is a child of the Spirit, while Ishmael is of the flesh (Galatians 4:28-29).

There is nothing spiritual in human faith. It's all about the senses (carnality) and is subject to failure and disappointment. On the contrary, God's kind of faith is supernatural because its object is the word, which is spirit and life; according to Christ (John 6:63).

If you desire to deal victoriously with impossibilities, what you need is the faith of God.

The difference between the two major kinds of faith available to man is very clear from the scriptures. While father Abraham trusted God and believed that the invisible word of God will produce the manifestation of the reality of his expectation (Isaac, the spiritual son); Thomas Didymus relied on his five senses to convince him of the reality of the resurrection of Christ. So Abraham exercised the faith of God while Thomas exhibited the sense-knowledge predominant faith of man.

It is important to grasp that the knowledge of the two major kinds of faith available to man, explains the tragedy of the non-functional and fruitless faith practiced by many. Many Christians are frustrated and defeated in their battle of faith because they only know and practice Thomas' sense-knowledge faith of man.

Other Cases of the Practice of the Faith of God:

Many powerful examples of people who successfully practiced God's kind of faith abound in the scriptures. A few of them are listed below:

1. *"By faith Noah, being warned of God of things not seen as yet, moved with fear, prepared an ark to the saving of his house; ...."* (Hebrews 11:7a KJV)

2. *"By faith Abraham, when he was called to go out into a place which he should after receive for an inheritance, obeyed; and he went out, not knowing whither he went."* (Heb 11:8).

3. *"Through faith also Sara herself received strength to conceive seed, and was delivered of a child when she was past age* (independent of physical evidence*), because she judged him faithful who had promised."* (Hebrews 11:11 KJV)

4. *"By faith the walls of Jericho fell down, after they were compassed about seven days."* (Hebrews 11:30 KJV)

5. *"By faith the harlot Rahaab perished not with them that believed not, when she had received the spies by faith."* (Heb. 11:31 KJV)

6. By God's kind of faith, *"Women received their dead raised to life again: and others were tortured, not accepting deliverance; that they might obtain a better resurrection:."* (Hebrews 11:35 KJV)

In Babylon, practicing God's kind of faith, Daniel did not focus on the den of lions; Shedrach, Meshach, and Abednego did not consider the hotness of the burning fiery furnace but they all trusted and believed God and His promises (word). By that they provoked divine intervention of the omnipotent God and were miraculously delivered.

What is the object of your faith? Man's action of faith will succeed or fail if the object of faith is based on anything (like human resources and ability) other than God and in His word.

Ten out of the twelve spies sent to investigate the Promised Land practiced the sense-knowledge faith of man (as they considered the magnitude of the giants). As a result they perished without reaching the Promised Land. On the contrary, Joshua and Caleb, practicing God's kind of faith, refused to be dominated by their senses (having seen that they were no match to the giants in the natural). Rather, they trusted in God, His words and promises, and became heroes. Their faith was productive, and they entered the Promised Land.

By God's kind of faith Queen Esther defied her king's protocol law of visitation and saved a generation of the Jews from a deadly holocaust. Space does not permit me to list many more examples. Please, do your own research and you will become more excited with God's kind of faith and perhaps be delivered from sense-knowledge faith of man if you are already a victim.

This faith trusts in God and acts on the Word of God independent of the senses and unfavorable hostile physical evidence.

God's kind of faith can be defined as trusting God and acting on His word irrespective of unfavorable circumstantial evidence. Hence-forth, our discussion on faith is only with reference to God's kind of faith.

CHAPTER 4
THE SOURCE OF FAITH

"**S**o *then faith cometh by hearing, and hearing by the word of God.*" (Romans 10:17 KJV)

It's amazing to note that faith does not come by prayer, fasting, praise and worship, or laying on of hands. Faith comes not only by knowing and memorizing the word but most importantly by hearing the word. In Romans 10:8, the Bible calls the word of God the word of faith. This signifies that the word of God is a massive container of faith. No word, no faith. For the purpose of emphasis, please note:

God's kind of faith can be defined as trusting God and acting on His word irrespective of unfavorable circumstantial evidence.

It is not only the word of God you know and have memorized (both exercise are required); but it is the word you will hear at the time of incident.

This is very important because faith is "a now phenomenon". It's a present event factor. Faith is never in the future. It's never futuristic. This is where many fail in their faith life-application. Hope is a future element, while faith is a present (now) force.

Many Christians are frustrated and defeated in their battle of faith because they only know and practice Thomas' sense-knowledge faith of man.

"Now faith is the substance of things hoped for, the evidence of things not seen."(Hebrews 11:1).

In 1 John 5:4, we see that our born-again (new birth) nature is also a vital significant source of our faith. Recall that we are partakers of the Divine Nature of God (11Peter1:4). This nature, among others (like righteousness, sanctification, holiness etc.), is also a nature of faith.

Now, let us consider how we can practically procure and release (practice) our faith in the face of challenging situations. The Bible clearly teaches that all believers in Christ are born again, spiritually victorious. And the weapon to activate and enforce our victory is our faith. Accordingly:

"For whatsoever is born of God overcometh the world: and this

is the victory that overcometh the world, even our faith." (I John 5:4 KJV)

The above scripture, without ambiguity, teaches the following lessons:

1. As a believer in Christ I'm born an over-comer.

2. As a believer in Christ I'm crowned and ordained a world over-comer. I'm not only predestined and predetermined to overcome the world and its wickedness (I John 5:19), but I've already accomplished that task through Christ. I'm not trying or struggling to overcome anything. The deal is done. Mission has been accomplished in the realm of the spirit by Christ and the victory credited to my account. What is left and needed is the enforcement of victory in the natural realm of existence by faith.

3. I'm also born victorious. Victory is in my DNA. I'm a partaker of the divine nature of God—DNA (II Peter 1:4). I'm not trying to be victorious, but I'm ordained and programmed victorious over the powers of darkness (Luke 10:19) and over unreasonable and wicked men and women who have no faith on earth (II Thessalonians 3:2).

4. As a born victorious over-comer, I'm supernaturally equipped with the weapon of faith (Romans 12:3; II Corinthians 4:13; Ephesians 2:8-9; Romans 10:8; II Peter 1:1) to enforce my victory in time of need. In other words, our spiritual birth came with the nature of faith. Romans 12:3 calls it the measure of faith. 11 Corinthians 4:13 calls

it the spirit of faith. Ephesians 2:8-9 calls it the gift of faith. Romans 10:8 calls it the word of faith. And 11 Peter 1:1 calls it *"like Precious Faith"*. How then do we practically procure and enforce our faith when we're provoked?

Faith is Voice Activated

Now, faith is! (Hebrews 11:1): If I'm in trouble now, I need to provoke, engage, and enforce the manifestation of my faith already in my nature (specifically, my spirit-man) now. But Romans 10:17 tells me that this faith can only come by hearing the word. Now, it is my responsibility to confess the relevant word of faith (believed in my heart). And when I do that, I will hear and when I hear my faith will automatically manifest and precipitate the needed victory which is already available to me in Christ Jesus. Jesus confirmed this in His teachings on faith:

"For verily I say unto you, if ye have faith as a grain of mustard seed, ye shall say unto this mountain. Remove hence to yonder place: and it shall remove; and nothing shall be impossible unto you" (Matthew17:20). See the following scriptures also:

"We having the same spirit of faith, according as it is written, I believed, and therefore have I spoken; we also believe, and therefore speak;" (II Corinthians 4:13 KJV)

"But the righteousness which is of faith speaketh on this wise, Say not in thine heart, Who shall ascend into heaven?" (Romans 10:6 KJV)

"But what saith it? The word is nigh thee, even in thy mouth, and in thy heart: that is, the word of faith which we preach;" (Romans 10:8 KJV)

Indeed, faith is a talking force. It speaks victory. Faith without your voice remains dormant, inactive (dead). What people call faith without the companion of voice is nothing but mental assent. *"That if thou shall confess with thy mouth the Lord Jesus, and shalt believe (faith) in thine heart that God hath raised him from the dead, thou shalt be saved."* (Romans 10:9 KJV)

The relevant word of faith you believe in your heart (spirit and soul - mind, will and emotion) must come out of your mouth (life and death storage) by the channel of confession. What you believe in your heart, you speak. That is the corresponding action of faith. "You believe and you speak".

"For with the heart man believeth (faith) unto righteousness; and with the mouth confession is made unto salvation." (Romans 10:10 KJV)

"That the communication of thy faith may become effectual by the acknowledging of every good thing which is in you in Christ Jesus." (Philemon 1:6 KJV). Acknowledgement here is the product of speaking. Whatever you believe must be actualized by speaking. The speaking dimension of practical faith is what is conspicuously missing in our faith lifestyle.

Faith comes not only by knowing and memorizing the word but most importantly by hearing the word.

Faith must be communicated out of the abundance of the promises of God. Effective and productive faith is a product of the confession of the promises of God. All the scriptures listed above simply show that faith is voice activated. Be sure to always add voice to your faith if you desire an effective productive lifestyle of the faith of the righteous.

CHAPTER 5
FAITH IS WARFARE

There is a truth that the devil does not want anybody to know, and that is the fact that our life struggles and challenges are spiritual conflicts master-minded by the devil, and his spiritual hosts of wickedness (including human agents of darkness). The natural man (non believer in Christ) and the carnal Christian cannot understand this, not to mention its acceptance. Nevertheless, it is a reality. Only the spiritual in Christ understands and prevails in this battle but the rest suffers needless casualties. To a believer, faith is a supernatural authoritative weapon for spiritual warfare against the kingdom of darkness.

Faith is Voice Activated.
No Word, No faith.

The Bible teaches that we gained entrance into the Kingdom of God by grace through faith and encourages us to walk and live in the same manner (Ephesians 2:8-9; Colossians 2:6-7: Galatians 3:11; Hebrews 10:38). Common sense shows that for the devil and his hosts to effectively oppose the children of God, they will have to oppose our faith. This is where our faith derived its nature of warfare and spiritual conflict. Satan does not want anybody to believe (or have faith) in God. He (Satan) wants us to worship him instead of God. Therefore, his primary motive of attacking and vanquishing our faith is to confine us to the realm or lifestyle that is independent of God. Recall that, that was the climax of his achievement in his assault against Adam and Eve in the Garden of Eden! Obviously, Satan successfully alienated Adam and Eve from God and plunged them into the dungeon of self and pride, as related to himself. Thus, Man died spiritually and became nothing but flesh. God Himself responded, saying: "My Spirit shall not always strive with man, for that he also is flesh"(Genesis6:3). God is a Spirit and they that worship him must worship (relate to) Him in spirit and in truth (the word of God) (John4:24).

Below are outstanding scriptures dealing with the conflict nature of faith.

"Beloved, when I gave all diligence to write unto you of the common salvation, it was needful for me to write unto you, and exhort you that ye should earnestly contend for the faith which was once delivered unto the saints." (Jude 1:3 KJV)

Our faith in Christ and His finished work on the cross is not only on fire by the forces of hell, but there is a fierce contention raging on against it! Subsequently, we must contend - fire for fire. The violent must take it by force (Matthew 11:12). Again, the Bible strongly admonished us as follows:

"Fight the good fight of faith, lay hold on eternal life, whereunto thou art also called, and hast professed a good profession before many witnesses." (I Timothy 6:12 KJV)

Carefully searching the scriptures we will discover that the fight of faith is the only fight we are commissioned and mandated to fight. And it's a good fight because we're not fighting for victory but from the victory advantage of the finished work on the cross by our Lord and Savior - Jesus Christ.

I am not trying to be victorious. I am ordained and programmed victorious over the powers of darkness.

As for the devil and his demons, we're not instructed to fight them but to resist them and to cast them out (James 4:7; I Peter 5:8-9; Matthew 10:1, 7-8; Mark 16:17-18). The devil and his hosts are defeated foes. Unfortunately, many of us spend our resources fighting a defeated enemy. I'd like to mention my seven D's of dominion over the devil. The devil is:

1. Defeated (Revelation 12:7-8)
2. Demoted (Revelation 12:8)
3. Dethroned (Revelation 12:8)
4. Displaced (Revelation 12:9-10; Luke 10:18)
5. Disarmed (Colossians 2:15)
6. Disgraced (Colossians 2:15)
7. Destroyed (Hebrews 2:14)

However, we must know that the devil is still active in the realm of darkness (Jude 6; II Peter 2:4). In fact, the Bible calls the devil and his demons rulers of the darkness of this world (Ephesians 6:12). Here we're dealing with spiritual darkness - where God does not operate. Sin, carnality, unbelief, fear, and many other vices constitute the realm of darkness. Of course, don't forget also that if you break the hedge, the serpent will bite you (Ecclesiastes 10:8).

Always be a doer of the work (James 1:25) - obeying and following divine instructions. To effectively, successfully and victoriously wage the warfare of faith; we must obey the following divine instructions:

1. Resist the devil whenever he seeks your attention (James 4:17).
2. Walk in the Spirit; always refusing to fulfill the lust of the flesh (Galatians 5:16).
3. Neither give place to the devil (Ephesians 4:27).
4. Abstain from all appearance of evil (I Thessalonians 5:22).
5. Be not overcome of evil, but overcome evil with God (Romans 12:21).
6. But put ye on the Lord Jesus Christ, and make no provision for the flesh to fulfill the lusts thereof (Romans 13:14).
7. Become a master in renewal of mind, taking thoughts captive, casting down imaginations and pulling down strongholds (Ephesians 4:22-23, Romans 12:1-2; II Corinthians 10:3-4). Because these are satanic induced - patterns of thinking that form fortified dwelling places for demons and demonic activities in our lives, excluding our

spirit man. These strongholds and imaginations are also ungodly and negative mindsets impregnated with hopelessness, and cause us to believe and accept a lie that the seemingly hopeless situations are unchangeable.

8. Learn how to put on the whole armor of God (Ephesians 6:10-18).

It must be emphasized that the warfare of faith has nothing to do with the direct confrontation and engagement with satanic forces, as many Christians do in the manner of spiritual warfare.

Again, this is not a call to fight Satan and his forces of evil. Such practices are nothing but obnoxious, offensive and repulsive displays of blatant unbelief towards the glorious finished work on the cross by our Lord and Savior, Jesus Christ. Remember! It is written: " it is finished" (John 14:30).

The warfare of faith has nothing to do with the direct confrontation and engagement with satanic forces, as many Christians do in the manner of spiritual warfare.

Our calling as "New Creation and Ambassadors of the Most High God, is to resist the devil and cast them out and heal all manner of sicknesses and diseases master-minded and perpetrated by them. (James 4:7, 1 Peter 5:8,9; Mark 16:17).

God's calling on our lives is a glorious, authentic and irrevocable mandate because we have been endued with power and authority over the devil. (Mathew 10:1,8; Luke 10:17-19)

35

The warfare of faith deals with the conflict between the manifestation of our redemptive benefits and the activities of our flesh and worldly challenging circumstances that tend to hinder us.

In another parlance, our unrenewed reasoning faculties, desires, feelings and senses wage war against God's plans, purpose and benefits of our salvation. Salvation is the greatest miracle of the ages. By this, the fallen man is completely delivered from the slavery of Satan, bondage, power, penalty of sin, bondage of Adamic origin and heritage and supernaturally (spiritually) recreated, and reconciled with His creator, and transferred into the family and kingdom of God.

The books of Jude 1:3 and 1 Timothy 6:12, vividly explain God's concept of the warfare of faith. Let us examine the scriptures again:

"Beloved, when I gave all diligence to write to you of the common salvation, it was needful for me to write unto you, and exhort you that ye should earnestly contend for the faith which was once delivered unto the saints." (Jude 1:3).

Here, we see that the faith mentioned has to do with our common salvation and not with the forces of darkness. Also 1 Timothy 6:12 declares:

"Fight the good fight of faith, lay hold on the eternal life to which you were called when you made your good confession in the presence of many witnesses."

Accordingly, the good fight of faith referred to has to do with our eternal life and not with Satan and his demons, witches, wizards and human agents of darkness. How did the church come up with this spiritual warfare of confrontation with the devil? The answer is in 1 Timothy 4:1.

Although the city of Ephesus was a satanic stronghold as recorded in the book of Acts, the Apostles and disciples did not engage the forces of darkness in a spiritual warfare. Rather, the Bible said, "So mightily grew the word of God and prevailed and many that believed came, and showed their deeds. Many of them also which used curious arts brought their books together, and burned them before all men: And they counted the price of them, and found it fifty thousand pieces of silver." (Acts19:19-20).

Please note unbiblical spiritual warfare of direct confrontation with the powers of darkness exposes practitioners to unprotected satanic attack which result to countless and needless casualties. The reason being that they plunge themselves into the realm of darkness of unbelief and, thereby, provoke the wrath of rulers of darkness of this world.

If you take another look at the scriptures of Jude 1:3 and 1 Timothy 6:12, you will discover that we (believers in Christ) are strongly exhorted to "earnestly contend" and also commanded to "fight the good fight of faith"—laying hold on our eternal salvation. 'Laying hold" is a strong militant command. Why is that so? The answer is that: "the flesh lusts against the Spirit, and the Spirit against the flesh; and they are contrary the one to the other; so that you cannot do the things that ye would", (Galatians 5:17).

Whatever rises up against us, to challenge what we have received and believed in Christ must be resisted with alacrity and acrimony.

I love the manner Hebrews 12:1 commented on the issue of warfare of faith after giving us exhaustive narrative of Spiritual and Biblical faith champions. It states:

"Wherefore seeing we also are compassed about with so great a cloud of witnesses, let us lay aside every weight, and the sin which doth so easily beset us, and let us run with patience the race that is set before us"

In other words, regardless of the unfavorable and offensive overwhelming circumstances of life; the word of grace that saturated and decorated us with salvation should always occupy the position of preeminence and final authority in our lives. This is the warfare or the good fight of faith. The faith of our common salvation must be defended even until death. Whatever rises up against us, to challenge what we have received and believed in Christ must be resisted with alacrity and acrimony. This is exactly what Adam and Eve failed to do when the devil tempted them in the garden of Eden.

The Bible says: "ye have not resisted unto blood, striving against sin". Also, "they overcame him (Satan), by the blood of the Lamb, and by the word of their testimony; and they loved not their lives unto death", (Hebrews 12:4; Revelation 12:11).

Finally, 11 Timothy 2:18 warns us that our faith can be overthrown. Please, make this confession now:

"Oh Lord, thank you for qualifying and enlisting me into the good fight of faith by the authority of the power of the Holy Ghost, who is working mightily in my life (Ephesians 3:20). I declare that my faith will not be overthrown, in the Mighty name of Jesus, Amen.

CHAPTER 6
FAITH IS THE LIFESTYLE OF THE RIGHTEOUS

O ne of the tragedies attempting to consume many Christians is lack of the knowledge of the truth that our eternal life (new creation, new life - Zoe, new birth, spiritual life), came with a new lifestyle of faith, righteousness, and holiness (Old things are passed away; behold all things have become new - II Corinthians 5:17).

"Having therefore brethren, boldness to enter into the holiest by the blood of Jesus,

By a new and living way, which he had consecrated for us, through the veil, that is to say, his flesh;" (Hebrews 10:19-20 KJV)

"For the love of Christ constraineth us; because we thus judge, that if one died for all, then were all dead. And that He died for all, that they which live should not henceforth live unto themselves, but unto Him which died for them, and rose again." (11 Corinthian 5:14, 15).

Truly our new spiritual life came with a new living way of the spirit, love, and faith. This refers to a supernatural lifestyle that is spotlessly dedicated to Christ; because, as Christ is, so are we in this world (1John4:17). We're admonished to live in the spirit, walk by faith without which no one can please God. By the same token we are to practice the love of God which is shed abroad in our hearts, because the nature of God is love. This nature we have received of Him (11 Peter 1:4).

What you believe in your heart, you speak. That is the corresponding action of faith. You believe and you speak.

Of course, space does not permit us here to address numerous scriptures that emphatically and strongly point to believers' corresponding heavenly lifestyle. But, suffice it to say that believers' lifestyle, inconsistent with our new nature, not only produces crises; but also creates open doors for insidious satanic assaults. It is written:

"Therefore we're buried with him (Christ) by baptism unto death: that like as Christ was raised up from the dead by the glory of the Father, even so we also should walk in newness of life." (Romans 6:4 KJV).

The emphasis here is on *"Newness of Life"*. This is important and interesting. Without any gainsaying, newness of life, demands newness of lifestyle. Truly, this is where Satan takes advantage of the righteous, because, many are blinded to this revelation truth that is responsible for freedom in Christ.

Through Christ Jesus, we received a new life and we are expected to walk in this new life (Life in the spirit). For to be carnally minded is death; but to be spiritually minded is life and peace (Romans 8:6). Also the spiritual man judges all things and nothing judges him (I Corinthians 2:15). Take a look at this scripture:

"For when we were in the flesh, the motions of sins, which were by the law, did work in our members to bring forth fruit unto death.

But now, we are delivered from the law, that being dead wherein we are held; that we should serve in <u>newness of spirit</u>, and not in the oldness of the letter." (Romans 7:5-6 KJV)

Again, the emphasis here is on spiritual lifestyle. We received new spirit when we became born again (Ezekiel 36:26; Romans 7:6); therefore, we must live and walk thereby accordingly. A lifestyle void of the spirit is responsible for the abundance of conflicts in the body of Christ, and as well as in many individuals.

"Behold, his soul which is lifted up is not upright in him: but the just shall <u>live by his faith</u>." (Habakkuk 2:4 KJV)

"For therein is the righteousness of God revealed from faith to faith: as it is written, The just shall <u>live by his faith</u>." (Romans 1:17 KJV)

"But that no man is justified by the law in the sight of God, it is evident: for the just shall <u>live by faith</u>." (Galatians 3:11 KJV)

"Now the just shall <u>live by faith</u>: but if any man draw back, my soul shall have no pleasure in him." (Hebrews 10:38 KJV)

In all these scriptures, God is stressing that His righteous ones are called to the lifestyle of faith. But *"...if any man draws back..."* <u>from the lifestyle of faith</u>, God himself declares that *"..my soul*

41

shall have no pleasure in him.." (Hebrews 10:38). Think about it! Here is another one:

"As ye have received Christ Jesus the Lord, so walk ye in him. Rooted and built up in him, and stablished in the faith, as ye have been taught, abounding therein with thanksgiving." (Colossians 2:6-7 KJV)

How did we receive Christ? We received Christ by grace through the walk of faith (Ephesians 2:8-9). The walk of faith enables us to appropriate what God has freely made available to us by the grace of our Lord Jesus Christ. Walking by faith is the same as walking in the spirit. Because faith comes by hearing the word of God; and the word is spirit and life (Romans 10:17; John 6:63).

The speaking dimension of practical faith is what is conspicuously missing in our faith life style.

Any Christian who is not living by faith is living a carnal lifestyle which is inconsistent with our new life, new spirit, new righteousness and new nature. Recall that our flesh (carnality) is waging war against our spirit (Galatians 5:17). Now, instead of resolving the conflict, we are aiding and abetting it by indulging in a carnal lifestyle. This is a strong issue that needs urgent resolution. You can now see the reason for unanswered prayers and powerlessness in the body of Christ today. The book of Romans is of great enlightenment in this issue:

"For to be carnally minded is death; but to be spiritually minded

is life and peace. Because the carnal mind is enmity against God: for it is not subject to the law of God, neither indeed can be. So then they that are in the flesh cannot please God. ...but if ye through the spirit do mortify the deeds of the body, ye shall live." (Romans 8:6-8, 13b KJV)

The lifestyle of faith is a spiritual lifestyle that begins with our ability to renew our minds on who we are in Christ (using the scriptures and the help of the Holy Spirit). Living by faith is entering into the rest of God (Hebrews 4:1-3). The unprecedented failures, short-comings, and weakness witnessed within the body of Christ are products of a lifestyle void of faith and the dominion of the Holy Spirit. This lifestyle is inconsistent with our new nature - the new creation life (I John 4:17).

Indeed, faith is a talking force. It speaks victory. Faith without your voice remains dormant, inactive (dead).

"If we live in the Spirit, let us also walk in the Spirit." (Galatians 5:25). This is to say that, a Spiritual life requires and demands a Spiritual lifestyle.

"This I say then, walk in the Spirit and ye shall not fulfill the lust of the flesh" (Galatians 5:16). The flesh (senses) is the greatest enemy of faith.

"For as many as are led by the Spirit of God, they are the sons of God." (Romans 8:14).

Without controversy, the benefits, authority, powers, rights and privileges associated with sonship in the Kingdom of God are mainly enjoyed by those who walk by faith and according to the Spirit. Unfortunately, the baby and carnal believers are:

(1) Subject to bondage under the hostile elements of this world (Galatians4: 3).

(2) Subject to the class of servants (denial of inheritance). And placed under tutors and governors until the time appointed of the father (Galatians4:1, 2).

(3) Subject to the capacity of ordinary (natural and powerless) men (1 Corinthians 3:3). Compare them with the Spiritual Man of 1 Corinthians 2:15; who judges all things and nothing judges him. He also has the capacity to operate the mind of Christ (1 Corinthians 2:16).

Without any gainsaying, newness of life, demands newness of lifestyle.

It's then compulsory and incumbent upon all believers to strive to live by faith, and consistently walk in the Spirit. This is the life style of the New Creation. This is what the Bible describes as:

"Put on the New Man, which after God is created in righteousness and true holiness." (Ephesians 4:24).

Walking *"worthy of the Lord unto all pleasing, being fruitful in every good work, and increasing in the knowledge of God"* (Colossians 1:10).

"For we are His workmanship, created in Christ Jesus unto good works, which God hath before ordained that we should walk in them." (Ephesians 2:10).

"For in Him we live, and move, and have our being; as certain also of your own poets have said. For we are also His offspring" (Acts 17:28).

Every believer in Christ is the substance, essence and product of Christ, because; God gave birth to us through Christ (James1:18):

"Of His (God) own will begat He us with the Word of truth (Christ), that we should be a kind of first fruits of His creation."

The summary of all these revelations is that Christ is our "Master Copy"; and we are His "Duplicates". This has been the heart-beat of God, even before the agenda of the first creation and the tragic generational incident of the Garden of Eden.

To a believer, faith is a supernatural, authoritative weapon for spiritual warfare against the kingdom of darkness.

Therefore, we must renew our minds with this truth and learn how to, *"put on the Lord Jesus Christ, and make not provision for the flesh, to fulfill the lusts thereof"* (Romans 13:14). *"Because as He (Christ) is, so are we in this world."* (1 John 4:17). This is the key to productive, successful, and victorious lifestyle of faith.

45

"For we walk by faith, not by sight", (2 Corinthians 5:7). Our New Creation walk is the walk of faith. Our victory, success, triumph and dominion of the planet earth; are products of our walk of faith. So, walk by faith!

Any lifestyle inconsistent with the faith of the righteous is an error that must be swiftly corrected to avoid spiritual, mental and physical conflict and defeat.

CHAPTER 7
FAITH IS A WEAPON

hy is it important to know that faith is a weapon? The answer to this question is very simple. For example, If you are carrying a physical weapon, it is obvious, and your consciousness of its availability enables you to use it where and when necessary. But this is not the case with faith.

Faith is the spiritual substance of our invisible expectation. It is the spiritual evidence of our unseen realities. Faith specializes in the unseen. If you can see the expectation, you don't need faith. Faith calls those things that be not as though they were, and downloads the unseen spiritual realities into physical manifestations. Therefore, faith is an invisible weapon. For instance:

"For the weapons of our warfare are not carnal, but mighty through God to the pulling down of strongholds;" (II Corinthians 10:4 KJV)

"Not carnal", means not visible, not natural and not physical.

These weapons are in no way related to the senses. Faith is among the weapons referred to above. It is a spiritual (invisible) but supernatural weapon of double dimension - offensive and defensive. In the book of Hebrews, we see that:

*"**By faith the walls of Jericho fell down, after they were compassed about seven days.**"* (Hebrews 11:30 KJV)

It is interesting to note that voice activated faith brought down the walls of Jericho. The existence and availability of physical massive weapons of warfare was not recognized or considered. This conquest of the most dreaded ancient fortress of the walls of Jericho and its inhabitants is fully recorded in Joshua 6:1-20.

Our faith in Christ and His finished work of the cross is not only on fire by the forces of hell, but there is a fierce contention raging on against it! Subsequently, we must contend - fire for fire.

The voice activated faith in the irrevocable divine instruction of God brought down the dreadful historic walls of Jericho. Also, the Word of faith spoken by Joshua (the servant of the Most High) enforced irrevocable curse on the city and inhabitants of Jericho to date, as shown below:

*"**And Joshua adjured them at that time, saying, Cursed be the man before the Lord, that riseth up and buildeth this city Jericho: he shall lay the foundation thereof in his first born, and***

in his youngest son shall he set up the gates of it." (Joshua 6:26 KJV)

This curse was fulfilled during the reign of King Ahab, years later and we see this recorded in I Kings 16:34 (KJV):

"In his days did Hiel the Beth-elite build Jericho: he laid the foundation thereof in Abiram his firstborn, and set up the gates thereof in his youngest son Segub, according to the word of the Lord, which he spake by Joshua the son of Nun."

That was what happened to Hiel when he attempted to rebuild the walls of Jericho. His first son, Abiram died when he laid the foundation, and when he set up the gates his youngest son, Segub died. Every Christian should be careful and sober in our utterances.

"O Lord our Lord, how excellent is thy name in all the earth! Who hast set thy glory above the heavens. Out of the mouth of babes and sucklings hast thou ordained strength because of thine enemies, that thou mightiest still the enemy and the avenger."(Psalm 8:1, 2).

The consequences of the unguarded use of our tongues are grievous, so we must be careful. If you have issues in this area your prayer should be *"Set a watch, O LORD, before my mouth; keep the door of my lips."* (Psalm 141:3 KJV).

God ordained power in our tongue as instrument of blessing to humanity and as a weapon against our enemies. The book of Proverbs clearly warned that:

"Death and life are in the power of the tongue: and they that love it shall eat the fruit thereof."(Proverbs 18:21).

It's amazing! Death and life are neither in the power of Satan and his host of wickedness nor in the hands of sickness and disease; but in the power of the tongue. Faith-filled word in the mouth of a Christian is as powerful as if God is speaking. This is not surprising because indeed, we stand as representatives or ambassadors of the kingdom of God (11 Corinthians 5:20). He speaks His word through us to rule, control and dominate the planet earth.

Jesus Himself taught: "*If you have faith as a grain of mustard seed, ye shall say unto this mountain. Remove hence to yonder place; and it shall remove; and nothing shall be impossible unto you.*" (Matthew17:20).

Above, faith stands as a devastating and mighty offensive weapon. For sure, whatever can move a mountain (representing obstacles of magnitude); is a mighty weapon.

Faith is the spiritual substance of our invisible expectation. It's the spiritual evidence of our unseen realities.

Furthermore, 1 John 5:4 also describes faith as a supernatural offensive weapon of victory for the born-again children of the Most High God.

"*For whatsoever is born of God overcometh the world: and this is the victory that overcometh the world, even our faith.*" (1 John 5:4 KJV)

Every Christian is born-again victorious. Victory is in our genes (1 John 4:4; 11 Corinthians 2:14;

1 Corinthians 15:57). But 1 John 5:4 above teaches that faith is the weapon with which we can launch, activate or enforce our victory. Why is that so? The reason is that we're beneficiaries and enforcers of the victory of Christ. Christ's victory on the cross over Satan and the forces of evil is credited to our (believers) accounts. Our identity in Christ guarantees our authority and gift of victory over the forces of evil. This victory, because it's in the past, though very much potent; must be activated by our faith according to 1 John 5:4. So, faith is our weapon of warfare to activate or provoke our victory in time of war (afflictions, temptations and oppressions).

But 1 Peter 5:8-9 explains that faith is a super defensive spiritual weapon against the devil and his hosts of wickedness.

"Be sober, be vigilant; because your adversary the devil, as a roaring lion, walketh about, seeking whom he may devour:

Whom resist stedfast in the faith, knowing that the same afflictions are accomplished in your brethren that are in the world." (I Peter 5:8-9 KJV)

The above divine instruction is: resist him relentlessly by faith. And don't forget, the battle originates in the mind and manifests in our life. The following lessons can be learned from this warfare passage of scriptures:

1. The devil has a catastrophic agenda to unleash similar afflictions on humanity.

2. The devil is described as an adversary (portraying a high level of antagonism) who operates with a style similar to a roaring lion (unprecedented scheme of intimidation). Fortunately, he's not a lion. "....*for he is a liar, and the*

father of it' (John 8:44c). We have only one lion of the tribe of Judah and His name is Jesus Christ. Prophet Jonah warned, saying: *"**They that observe lying vanities forsake their own mercy.**"* (Jonah 2:8). Please learn how to trash his relentless assault of deception in your mind. Develop a `sober mindset (serious-mindedness) that will always enable you to swiftly arrest any satanic program of deception in your mind.

God ordained power in our tongue as instrument of blessing to humanity and as a weapon against our enemies.

---

3. The devil seeks whom he may devour. That means he lacks the capacity to devour everybody. He can only successfully devour those who cannot resist him by faith. Faith pleases God but destroys the devil and his insidious and relentless assault of deception in the minds of people (no exemption). If you ignore him, you have identified with the needless casualties. Hallelujah! Glory be to God.

4. We're advised to be sober (serious-minded, clear-headed, self-controlled) and vigilant (alert) because of his craftiness which he unleashes via relentless assaults of deception in people's minds. The Bible teaches that Satan and his seducing spirits specialize in corrupting our minds as follows:

*"**But I fear, lest by any means, as the serpent beguiled***

Eve through his subtilty, so your minds should be corrupted from the simplicity that is in Christ."(11 Corinthians 11:3).

"Now the Spirit speaketh expressly, that in the latter times some shall depart from the faith, giving heed to seducing spirits, and doctrines of devils". (1Timothy 4:1).

In these scriptures, we see that Satan's agenda is to corrupt our minds, while his demons are delegated to also seduce our minds. What else do we need to know about our invisible battles? The Bible says: as a man thinks in his heart, so shall he be. This is to say that all the negative, fearful, ungodly and sinful thoughts; plaguing our minds and dominating and plunging our lives into destruction, are master minded by Satan and his demons. According to 11 Corinthians 10:3-5; these thoughts eventually become strongholds, which are:

(a) mindsets impregnated with hopelessness and also causes people to believe and accept a lie that these seemingly hopeless situations are unchangeable.

(b) Also, satanic induced patterns of thinking that have become fortresses for habitation (dwelling places) of demons and demonic activities in the lives of people.

"For though we walk in the flesh, we do not war after the flesh; (For the weapons of our warfare are not carnal, but mighty through God to the pulling down of strongholds;) Casting down imaginations, and every high thing that exalteth itself against the knowledge of God, and bringing into captivity every thought to the obedience of Christ. "(11 Corinthians 10:3-5).

5. We're admonished to resist him <u>steadfastly</u> by the finished work on the cross because we already have victory over him (Satan) through our Lord Jesus Christ. Here, we're required to enforce this delegated victory over Him steadfastly (without ceasing). Whenever we overcome him, we must remain in vigilant expectation of his return. He is desperate and hence ferocious because his time is short as we read in Revelation 12:12 quoted below:

"Therefore rejoice, ye heavens, and ye that dwell in them. Woe to the inhabiters of the earth and of the sea! for the devil is come down unto you, having great wrath, because he knoweth that he hath but a short time."

FAITH AS AN ARMOR:

Faith is described as a powerful armor of defense in the semblance of a huge shield.

"Above all, taking the shield of faith, wherewith ye shall be able to quench all the fiery darts of the wicked." (Ephesians 6:16 KJV)

I like to ask questions to illustrate my point. If faith is what is needed to abort fiery darts of the devil, what are the fiery darts that the devil is shooting against us? Obviously, they should be the opposite of faith which are doubts, unbelief and lies (error). We can see that the fiery darts are spiritual (invisible) by nature. So we use the armor of faith to knock out missiles of satanic doubts and unbelief. Faith therefore is believers' spiritual authority.

It's interesting to know that faith is a powerful weapon at our disposal. But it's most important to know how to practically launch or release our faith in the day of adversity. The Bible clearly teaches us how to use our faith briefly as follows. Please note that these were fully discussed previously, but repetition is an advantage:

1. "*...If you have __faith__ as a grain of mustard seed, ye shall say unto this mountain, remove hence to yonder place; and it shall remove; and nothing shall be impossible unto you.*" (Matthew 17:20 KJV)

2. "*....If you have __faith__ and doubt not, ye shall not only do this which is done to the fig tree, but also you shall say unto this mountain, Be thou removed, and be thou cast into the sea; it shall be done.*" (Matthew 21:21 KJV).

3. "*For verily I say unto, That whosoever shall say unto this mountain, be thou removed, and be thou cast into the sea; and shall not doubt in his heart , but shall believe that those things which he saith shall come to pass; he shall have whatsoever he saith.*"(Mark11:23). Note that he shall have whatever he says, other factors withstanding.

4. "*We having the same __spirit of faith__, according as it's written, I believed, therefore have I spoken: we also believe and therefore speak.*" (11 Corinthians 4:13 KJV)

Considering the scriptures above, a combination of the word and your tongue will raise up a standard against your enemies. Please, do not go after your giant (enemies, challenges) with your mouth closed. All the scriptures above teach that faith is voice-activated. Operative productive faith places a demand on our voice. No voice, no faith as stated earlier.

It's interesting to know that faith is a powerful weapon at our disposal. But it's most important to know how to practically launch or release our faith in the day of adversity.

Even Romans 10:17 confirms that faith comes by hearing the word. It follows that if we have faith, the next step of action will be to confess (speak) the relevant word of faith. This is also confirmed in Romans 10:8 which declares:

"The word is nigh thee, even in thy mouth, and in thy heart: that is; the word of faith, which we preach."

Speak the word, and speak the word. No plan 'B' is required. Learn from the Roman Centurion who made a demand on Jesus saying: *"Speak the word only..."* (Matthew 8:8)

In conclusion, in order to release (use) your faith in the face of adversity, please, follow the following steps:

Step One:

As a new creation, remember that you're a beneficiary of the victory accomplished in the finished work on the cross by Christ Jesus (John 19:30; 1 Corinthians 15:57; 11 Corinthians 2:14; 1 John 5:4). You received the gift of victory the day you became born again.

Step Two:

Notice that faith is the weapon to enforce your victory as an over-comer (1 John 5:4). You are born an over comer and saturated with victory. Victory is in your gene. You cannot be separated from victory.

Faith, therefore, is the believer's spiritual authority.

Step Three:

Do not forget the source of the manifestation of your faith. Faith comes by hearing the word. You must speak in order to hear and receive as well.

Step Four:

Then open your mouth and speak the relevant word of faith so that you can hear. Even your adversary who cannot survive the word will hear.

These simple steps and procedure will frustrate the devices of your enemies so that they will not be able to perform their enterprise against you (Job 5:12). Moreover, no weapon fashioned against you will prosper and any tongue that will rise up against you, you can always condemn with the word of faith in your mouth (Isaiah 54:17).

CHAPTER 8
THE LEGALITY OF FAITH

Faith is a legislative agenda which God instituted to guide, drive and direct the lifestyle (including battles) of His offsprings and members of His family called the household of faith (Galatians 6:10).

"AS we have therefore opportunity, let us do good unto all men, especially unto them who are of the household of faith." (Galatians 6:10).

Notice that the family of God is called the household of faith.

Faith is a spiritual law of the kingdom of God and the righteousness of God, as stated below:

"Where is boasting then? It's excluded. By what law? of works? Nay: but by the law of faith." (Romans 3:27 KJV)

Why is it important to know that faith is a law? Law is a regulator. It's the will of God that all His children will operate a uniform lifestyle: since we have the same spirit, nature, and righteousness.

As a result, there must be orderliness and uniformity in our lifestyle, principles, and conditions by which we can appropriate and apprehend our inheritance in Christ (Colossians 1:12). The Bible describes this inheritance as everlasting inheritance (Hebrews 9:15).

However, the most important lesson to learn about the legal dimension of faith is that: a law has the power to regulate situations and the potential to override other laws.

Therefore, you that have received the gift and the measure of the faith of Christ, you must be confident and rest assured that the operation of your faith will arrest and put to an end any situation contrary to the will of God. Remember also that the law of lift overrides the law of gravity. Learn how to use the law of faith to override the agenda of your enemies.

The most important lesson to learn about the legal dimension of faith is that: a law has the power to regulate situations and the potential to override other laws.

It is very encouraging to be acquainted with the following revelation:

(1) *"Thine, O Lord is the greatness, and the power, and the glory, and the victory, and the majesty: for all that is in the heaven and in the earth is thine; thine is the kingdom, O Lord, and thou art exalted as head above all. Both riches and honour come of thee, and thou reignest over all; and in thine hand is power and*

might; and in thine hand it is to make great, and to give strength unto all"(1 Chronicles 29:11).

(2)"The Lord hath prepared his throne in the heavens; and his kingdom ruleth over all."(Psalms 103:19).

(3)"Now unto Him (God) that is able to do exceeding abundantly above all that we ask or think, according to the power that worketh in us."(Ephesians 3:20).

The Almighty God, the one who has all the power, greatness, might and dominion; the one who can do all things righteous: He's the one who legislated the law of faith to enable us exercise His kind of dominion in this world.

We are in this kingdom that rules over all other kingdoms, and this kingdom is in us, (Luke 17:21; Colossians 1:13). We have the supernatural keys of this kingdom (Matthew 16:19). The Spirit that drives this kingdom is permanently dwelling in us. (1 Corinthians 6:19). Moreover, we are the recipients of the law of faith by which God calls the things that be not as though they were (Romans 4:17; 12:3; 11 Corinthians 4:13; Colossians 2:12).

CHAPTER 9
THE RELATIONSHIP BETWEEN
FAITH, BELIEF, AND RECEIVE

A ny process of faith, which does not incorporate believing and receiving is not a real faith (Bible faith - God's kind of faith). Such faith can be classified as mental accent faith or sense knowledge faith (human faith). Also, lack of the knowledge of the difference between faith and belief hinders the effectiveness and productivity of our faith lifestyle.

Hebrews 11:1 defined faith as a substance and also as an evidence. Both substance and evidence are nouns - the name of a thing in this instance. However, Mark 11:24 describes belief as a verb (corresponding action of faith) as well as receiving. Take a look!

"...What things so ever ye desire, when ye pray, believe that ye receive them, and ye shall have them." (Mark 11:24 KJV)

"Believe that ye receive them and ye shall have them." This phrase is what I regard as the mystery of the practice of faith, and it simply reveals that believing is receiving and receiving is having. In other words, the moment you believe (corresponding

action of faith), you have received and you will experience the manifestation of your expectation.

Remember that faith deals with the unseen realities (unseen realities in the sense that they exist in the spirit (invisible) realm). They represent our spiritual blessings in the heavenly places in Christ (Ephesians 1:3). By the assistance of the Holy Spirit, 11 Peter 1:3 explained the spiritual blessings as "*...all things that pertain unto life and godliness,..*".

The things associated with godliness are things that help us to be like God (please note: not to be God but like God) and function like God; since we are recreated in His image, likeness and spiritual nature (Ephesians 4:21-32; Galatians 4:1-7; 11 Peter 1:4; 1 John 4:17; 1 Corinthians 3:16; 11 Corinthian 6:16, 18). Life in 11 Peter 1:3, refers to the Life of God (Zoë)

Lack of the knowledge of the difference between faith and belief hinders the effectiveness and productivity of our faith lifestyle.

Faith is a spirit, dealing with the unseen which is expected to become visible - calling the things that be not as though they were (Romans 4:17). Believing and waiting to receive is hope. There is no faith in that. Faith is believing and receiving, according to Mark 11:24.

The moment you believed, you have received. This is independent of sense knowledge.

Believing (corresponding action of faith) = Receiving and Receiving = Having (i.e. the manifestation of my expectation).

Believing is receiving and receiving is having (manifestation). Again, the moment you believe you have received, whether there is physical evidence or not. We're not moved by sight but by our belief. We are moved by what we believe (the word of God and His promises). If we experience instantaneous manifestation of our expectation, when we release our faith; that is a miracle. Otherwise, we must believe and patiently wait for the manifestation.

How Important is Faith?

"In the beginning God created the heaven and the earth." (Genesis 1:1 KJV). How did He do that?

"And God said, Let there be light: and there was light." (Genesis 1:3 KJV).

"Through faith we understand that the worlds were framed by the word of God, so that things which are seen were not made of things which do appear." (Hebrews 11:3 KJV)

In all His creation we see the God of faith calling those things that be not as though they were. In addition to these scriptures there are many others which altogether reveal that the universe with its complexities and supernatural faculty was designed, crafted, and executed by God through faith. Humanity also is the product of God's word of faith. *"And God said, Let us make man in our image, after our likeness:..."* (Genesis 1:26 KJV)

God spoke man into existence before He got busy with the mud in Genesis 2:7. It's also very exciting to note that Christ and the new creation who went to the cross with Him, died with Him, buried with Him, were altogether raised into newness of life and newness of spirit by the faith of God.

"Buried with him in baptism, wherein as ye are risen with him through the faith of the operation of God, who hath raised him from the dead." (Colossians 2:12 KJV)

The faith of the operation of God raised us together with Christ from the dead supernaturally. So in creation and recreation God exercised His faith. Clearly, without faith, man will be lost forever without reconciliation, restoration, and relationship with His creator (God). Without faith no one can approach God, be reconciled with God, or exercise a meaningful relationship with God. Galatians 3:26 makes this very clear: *"For ye are all the children of God by faith in Christ Jesus."*

This is also the same with John 1:12: *"But as many as received him, to them gave he power to become the sons of God, even to them that believe (that is have faith) on his name:"*

In conclusion humanity is the product of faith. Therefore, we exist by faith and are expected to live by faith.

"For in Him (Word of Faith) we live, and move, and have our being; as certain also of your own poets have said, for we are also His offspring." (Acts17:28).

CHAPTER 10
GRACE AND FAITH

The presence of the unification of grace and faith in the Kingdom of God constitute the foundation of God's redemptive agenda for humanity. Grace and faith are inseparable in God's relationship with the redeemed. This is true because Christ is located in both grace and faith.

"For the grace (Jesus) of God that bringeth salvation hath appeared to all men," (Titus 2:11 KJV)

"The grace of the Lord Jesus Christ, and the love of God, and the communion of the Holy Ghost, be with you all. Amen." (11 Corinthians 13:14 KJV)

Although we popularly define grace as unmerited favor of God, which I'm not disputing, actually, grace is Christ by Biblical inspiration.

From Titus 2:11 we note that Christ is the grace of God that brought salvation to mankind. He offered Himself as a gift to us and as an offering and a sacrifice to God for a sweet smelling savor (Ephesians 5:2).

Christ is the Word of God and the word of God is the word of faith, and faith comes by hearing the word; therefore, Christ is our faith.

From 11 Corinthians 13:14 we observe that Christ is the embodiment of the grace and love of God. Christ cannot be separated from grace. Indeed, He is the personality of the grace of God.

"For God so loved the world, that he gave his only begotten Son (the grace of God), that whosoever believeth in him should not perish, but have everlasting life." (John 3:16 KJV)

Indeed, Christ is located in Grace. Christ is also conspicuously located in Faith as shown by many scriptures as follows:

"So then faith cometh by hearing, and hearing by the word of God." (Romans 10:17).

Romans 10:8 also calls the word of God, the word of faith. No doubt, the word of God is the divine source of faith. However, many scriptures declare that Christ is the word of God. If Christ is the word of God, He is also the word of faith. The following scriptures indicate that Christ is the word of God, who is also called the Word Of Faith

"In the beginning was the Word, and the Word was with God, and the Word was God.

And the word was made flesh (Christ), *and dwelt among us, (and we beheld his glory, the glory as of the only begotten of the Father), full of grace and truth."* (John 1:1, 14 KJV). No doubt, Jesus is the word made flesh, and full of grace and truth (the Word)

Also, Revelation 19:13 declares that the name of Jesus is the Word of God. Even 1John 5:7, dealing with the GODHEAD and the triunion (Trinity) nature of God, throws more light:

"For there are three that bear record in heaven, the Father, the Word, and the Holy Ghost: and these three are one."

Since Christ is the Word of God and the Word of God is the word of faith, and faith comes by hearing the word; therefore, Christ is our faith. We can see why some scriptures in the epistle describe our faith as the faith of Christ (Galatians 2:16, 20; Romans 3:22). Also, Hebrews 12:2 declares that Jesus is the author and finisher of our faith. Scriptures abound, testifying that Christ is the source, supplier and consummation of our faith. This decorates our faith with a divine nature and capacity to disgrace our enemies and break the power of impossibility if properly enforced.

"We having the same spirit of faith..."

(11 Corinthians 4: 13). It's very encouraging to learn that the faith of a believer is supernatural (Spirit of faith). We are not operating a natural human faith that is not reliable or subject to chance, circumstances and situations.

In summary, Christ is our grace as well as our faith and both (grace

69

and faith) are our supernatural free gifts from God. Most importantly, Romans 5:1-2 explains that without a supernatural combination of the grace and faith of Christ, fallen man has no place in God.

"Therefore being justified by FAITH, we have peace with God through our Lord Jesus Christ: By whom also we have access by FAITH into this GRACE wherein we stand, and rejoice in hope of the glory of God."

In the above scripture, faith conspicuously stands as a spiritual instrument to appropriate (take hold of) all that God has freely given to us by His Grace (1 Corinthians 2: 12).

"Therefore it is of FAITH, that it might be by GRACE; to the end the promise might be sure to all the seed; ..." (Romans 4:16).

Without Grace, Faith has nothing to possess and account to the redeemed; and without Faith; Grace remains inaccessible to the redeemed.

"For by grace are ye saved through faith; and that not of yourselves: it is the gift of God:" (Ephesians 2:8-9 KJV).

Salvation therefore, is the product of a supernatural combination of the activities of Grace and Faith. The importance of Grace and Faith in the eternal destiny of mankind cannot be over emphasized:

(1) Grace and Faith stand between God's everlasting redemptive plan and the fallen old creature (unbeliever) (Ephesians 2: 8-9).

(2) Grace and Faith also stand between the everlasting inheritance of the Saints and the righteous new creature (11 Corinthians 4:15; Romans 4:16). The inheritance of the

believer is a product of the Grace of God. But Faith is the instrument of possession.

Humanity will for ever be grateful to God for many things, especially the truth that Grace and Faith are gifts from on high. If both of them were to be earned (products of work), humanity would for ever be lost. This is true because none will qualify.

Faith conspicuously stands as a spiritual instrument to appropriate (take hold of) all that God has freely given to us by His Grace.

The important lesson to learn from this exposition of the union of grace and faith is that you cannot successfully benefit from any of them without striking a judicious balance between them (grace and faith). Many struggle in their walk and practice of faith because they do not incorporate the grace of God. Faith and grace are the supernatural currency in the Kingdom of God. Faith enables us to appropriate and take hold of all that God has freely made available to us by grace. Let us have a second look at Romans 5: 1-2.

"Therefore being justified by faith, we have peace with God through our Lord Jesus Christ:

By whom also we have access by faith into this grace wherein we stand, and rejoice in hope of the glory of God." (Romans 5:1-2 KJV)

Grace and faith; what a significant, supernatural combination?

By faith we have access into the grace of God which is the embodiment of the glory of God. Can you see that the only access to the abundant grace of God is faith? Though the grace of God is free, God requires us to come with faith to appropriate all that He has freely given to us (11 Corinthians 2:12; Romans 8:32;

11 Corinthians 4:15; 1 Corinthians 3:21-23).

Without grace there will be no need for faith. Absence of grace requires the presence of the law as in the Old Testament (covenant). And the presence of the law requires works instead of faith. But without faith, no one will take advantage of the grace of God. A detailed analysis of Romans 4: 16 will be helpful.

"Therefore it is of faith, that it might be by grace; to the end the promise might be sure to all the seed (Abraham's seed - Christ - which includes all believers - Gentiles and Jews)*; not to that only which is of the law, but to that also which is of the faith of Abraham; who is the father of us all."* (Romans 4:16 KJV)

This scripture is very easy to understand. It simply says:

1. That the promise that God made to Abraham and his seed (and that is the ownership of the whole world - Romans 4:13) is not only for the Jewish descendants but also for Gentile believers in Christ (Galatians 3:29).

2. That because God gave it (heir of the world) to Abraham by grace (free - independent of works) it must be appropriated by faith by his children.

"For the promise, that he (Abraham) *should be the heir of the world, was not to Abraham, or to his seed, through the law*

(works), *but through the righteousness of faith.*" (Romans 4:13 KJV)

Unfortunately, many believers have no knowledge of this truth that God willed the whole world to Abraham and his seed. Cultivating the mindset that God had provided all your needs by grace will enable you to successfully and productively practice your faith without room for doubt and unbelief. This is true because: "*God is able to make all grace abound toward you; that ye, always having all sufficiency in all things, may abound to every good work.*" (11 Corinthians 9:8)

All sufficiency in all things pertaining to life and godliness are available to the New Creation by Grace through Faith. Take a look at this:

"*Not that we are sufficient of ourselves to think any thing as of ourselves; but our sufficiency is of God.*"(11 Corinthians 3: 5).

The sufficiency of God is a product of the Grace of God, but the manifestation is incumbent on Faith. Grace must be balanced with Faith. The sufficiency of God must be appropriated by faith.

Please do not forget:

".... *It is of Faith, that it might be by Grace; to the end the promise might be sure to all the seed...*" (Romans 4: 16). This scripture is very significant in the analysis of the balance of Grace and Faith. The emphasis is that the promise to the Seed (Christ-incorporating both Jews and Gentile believers -Galatians 3:29), came from God through the agency of Grace. Therefore, the promise must be appropriated by faith.

"*And if ye be Christ's, then are ye Abraham's seed, and heirs according to the promise*" (Galatians 3:29).

PART II
ROOTS AND PILLARS
OF FAITH

BACKGROUND INFORMATION

Accordingly, as severally emphasized in some areas in this book, the knowledge of the will of God refers to the word of God. And spiritual understanding refers to the ability of the Holy Spirit to enlighten the eyes of our understanding, and enable us to assimilate the true meaning of the word of God. Wisdom generally signifies the application of the word of God. An effective lifestyle of faith by the righteous demands adequate knowledge, understanding, and wisdom of the roots and pillars of faith.

The sufficiency of God is a product of the Grace of God, but the manifestation is incumbent on Faith.

The roots and pillars of faith in this discourse refers to the elements that constitute the foundation of faith. There are too many to be accommodated in this book, thus suffice it to mention but just a few. Endless struggles take place in the lifestyle of faith as it is surrounded by inadequate knowledge, understanding, and wisdom of the following elements (to be discussed in the following chapters) which constitute the roots and pillars of faith.

CHAPTER 11
THE ALMIGHTY GOD - THE ROOT AND PILLAR OF OUR FAITH

The root and pillar of the faith of the righteous is the Almighty and everlasting God. Some writers and preachers describe Him as the object of our faith. If the object of your faith is not God, then you're not practicing the faith of God. You're practicing human faith, which is unreliable.

Some people drive through a traffic light when it turns green simply because they believe and trust that the opposing traffic will yield to the red signal instructing them to stop. But we all know that this is not always the case. In this scenario, the object of their faith is not God but their own judgment of the integrity of other road users in obeying traffic regulations.

The same situation is applicable to many who fly in airplanes, trusting the safety standard and reputation of the airlines, their pilots, and staff. Some write examinations basing their faith in their intellectual ability and hard work. And many exercise great faith in their personal physicians, and the prescribed medications they take.

In a certain Christian program, I heard the preacher tenaciously and consistently proclaiming that his success in ministry was because of his spiritual human father. Time and again he attributed the success of his explosive, and prophetic ministry to the anointing transferred to him by his earthly spiritual father and mentor. He encouraged the listening audience to connect with the minister who was present in the conference. He never at any time mentioned God as his source. He gave all the glory to a man, who lives at the discretion and mercy of the living God.

If all that we do is based on anything other than God, then our faith is subject to corruption and disappointment. This kind of faith can be labeled as subjective and not objective. The Psalmist declared: *"In thee, O Lord, do I put my trust."* (Psalm 71:1a KJV)

And Joseph also declared: *"...how then can I do this great wickedness, and sin against God?"* (Genesis 39:9c KJV). Also the Bible said, whatever we do without faith in God is tantamount to sin (Romans 14:23). God remains the foundation and object of the faith that is productive, incorruptible, and irrevocable. Furthermore, we read in Romans:

"For what if some did not believe? shall their unbelief make the faith of God without effect? God forbid: yea, let God be true, but every man a liar; as it is written, That you mightiest be justified in thy sayings, and mightiest overcome when thou art judged." (Romans 3:3-4KJV)

The scripture above simply declares that because God is the root and pillar of the faith we practice, our faith is effective as God guarantees our justification (righteousness) and victory. In other words, our righteousness (right standing with God) and victory in life are the products of faith rooted in unflinching trust in God.

Elizabeth the mother of John the Baptist prophesied to Mary (the mother of Jesus) saying:

"And blessed is she that believed: for there shall be a performance of those things which are told her from the Lord." (Luke 1:45 KJV)

She unequivocally confirmed that faith which its root and pillar is the Most High God, provokes the manifestation of the promises of God.

To corroborate the subject matter, Jesus, on the occasion of the seemingly tragic and later miraculous death of Lazarus, addressed Martha saying: *"Did I not tell you that if you believe, you will see the glory of God?"* (John 11:40 NIV)

This is also a confirmation of what the Bible said in Romans 5:2 that access to the supernatural grace of God; which is the inexhaustible storage of the blessings of God, is only by faith in God. That is, faith which its root and pillar is the God of our Lord Jesus Christ, the father of glory, in whom the whole family in heaven and earth are named (Ephesians 3:15 KJV).

If all that we do is based on anything other than God, then our faith is subject to corruption and disappointment.

Again, Jesus, lovingly cautioned the father of the epileptic lad saying: *"If thou canst believe* (in God), *all things are possible to him that believeth."* (Mark 9:23 KJV). Truly, the power of impossibility is broken and terminated by faith which is rooted in our God. When next you launch your faith, cultivate the consciousness that the root and pillar of your faith is the omnipotent God. And you will neither be ashamed nor disappointed.

Remember: "*Faithful, is He* (God) *that calleth you, who also will do it.*" (1 Thessalonians 5:24 KJV). He is a faithful God. He is "not a man, that he should lie; neither the son of man, that he should repent: hath he said, and shall he not do it? or hath he spoken, and shall he not make it good? (Numbers 23:19). In Psalm 89:34, he declared:

"*My covenant (promises) will I not break, nor alter the thing that is gone out of my lips.*".

Assuredly, faith rooted and grounded in God and His promises can not be annulled. The power of uncertainty in this atmosphere of trust is broken.

Without any gainsaying, our God is a God of faith who calls: "*...those things which be not as though they were*" (Romans 4:17 KJV). He also programmed his offspring (the redeemed humanity) to live and to please him by faith, saying: "*And my righteous ones will live by faith. But I will take no pleasure in anyone who turns away.*"(Hebrews 10:38 NLT). And also without faith it is impossible to please Him (Hebrews 11:6 KJV)

Our God is a God of faith who calls: "...those things which be not as though they were."

This follows that God-ordained lifestyle of the righteous (believer in Christ), is the lifestyle of faith which is rooted and grounded in God and His word (promises). Without this dimension of faith, it's impossible to please God.

After Jesus' triumphant entry to Jerusalem, he took a journey to the city of Bethany with his disciples. On their return journey to Jerusalem, he confronted a fig tree and cursed it because he found no fruit on the tree. The following day, as they departed from Jerusalem, traveling through the same route; Peter called the attention of Jesus to the fact that the cursed fig tree had withered. Notice the response of Jesus:

"...and Jesus answering saith unto them, have faith in God." (Mark 11:22). Although the correct interpretation would have been "have God's kind of faith", however, Christ's exposition here is that every irrevocable and infallible faith, must be anchored and rooted in God.

CHAPTER 12
CHRIST - THE ROOT AND PILLAR
OF OUR FAITH

One glorious day the multitude was searching for Jesus and the Bible narrated:

"When the people therefore saw that Jesus was not there, neither His disciples, they also took shipping, and came to Capernaum, seeking for Jesus.

And when they had found him on the other side of the sea, they said unto him, Rabbi, when camest thou hither?

Jesus answered them and said, Verily, verily, I say unto you, Ye seek me, not because ye saw the miracles, but because ye did eat of the loaves, and were filled.

Labour not for the meat which perisheth, but for that meat which endureth unto everlasting life, which the Son of man shall give unto you: for him hath God the Father sealed.

Then said they unto him, What shall we do that we might work the works of God?

Jesus answered and said unto them, This is the work of God that ye believe on him whom he hath sent." (John 6:24-29 KJV).

To do the work of God, to be approved of God, to be reconciled with God, to be recreated and begotten of God in Christ Jesus into His glorious household, you must believe (have faith) in Christ whom God sent for the propitiation of the sins of mankind and the redemption of man. Christ, in His role as our redeemer, became the root and pillar of our faith. Without Christ there will be no productive faith in God, and no infallible faith in life.

Hebrews 12:1-3 crowned Him the author and finisher of our faith. He became the originator and perfection of our faith. The Bible cautioned us to focus on Him, lest we will be weary and faint in our unregenerate mind (a mind that is not born again). This mind must be renewed.

Without Christ there will be no productive faith in God, and no infallible faith in life.

As a believer in Christ, who and what is the object of your faith? What do you consider as the root and pillar of your faith? Whenever you exercise your faith, do you focus on Christ - the author and finisher of our faith? Or, do you focus on your self-righteousness, holiness, and personal resources? Some might even focus on people, apostles, and prophets! Some, their focus might be on spiritual fathers, leaders, and mentors. Any attempt to practice faith independent of God and Christ might lead to failure and frustration. God himself delegated the foundation (root and pillar) of our faith to Christ. In the book of John chapter 3, verse 16 (KJV), the Bible declares:

"For God so loved the world that he gave his only begotten Son, that whosoever believeth in him should not perish, but have everlasting life."

Believing in Christ, which is the corresponding action of faith in Christ (the faith of Jesus Christ - God's kind of faith) accordingly, qualifies anyone to receive the everlasting life of God. Jesus Himself confirmed this when He said:

"The thief cometh not, but for to steal, and to kill, and to destroy: I am come that they might have life, and that they might have it more abundantly." (John 10:10 KJV)

Concerning mighty miracles, signs, and wonders, the Bible has these to say from Apostle Paul:

"And I, brethren, when I came to you, came not with excellency of speech or of wisdom, declaring onto you the testimony of God.

For I determined not to know anything among you, save Jesus Christ, and him crucified.

And I was with you in weakness, and in fear, and in much trembling.

And my speech and my preaching was not with enticing words of man's wisdom, but in demonstration of the spirit and of power:

That your faith should not stand in the wisdom of men, but in the power of God." (I Corinthians 2:1-5 KJV)

"Through mighty signs and wonders, by the power of the Spirit

of God; so that from Jerusalem, and round about unto Illyricum, I have fully preached the Gospel of Christ." (Romans 15:19 KJV)

How was Paul able to be associated with mighty signs and wonders, miracles and the miraculous? We know that miracles are the products of faith as stated by (Galatians 3:5):

"He therefore that ministereth to you the spirit, and worketh miracles among you, doeth he it by the works of the law, or by the hearing of faith."

What kind of faith did Apostle Paul operate? What was the root and pillar of his faith? I suppose, Galatians 2:20 (KJV) provides the answers to this:

"I am crucified with Christ: nevertheless I live; yet not I, but Christ liveth in me: and the life which I now live in the flesh I live by the faith of the Son of God, who loved me, and gave himself for me."

"I live by the faith of the son (Christ) of God, who loved me, and gave himself for me." Without ado, Apostle Paul by the inspiration of the Holy Spirit declares that the root of his faith was Christ.

Obviously, the root and pillar of the faith of Apostle Paul was Jesus Christ. And the kind of faith he (Paul) operated was the faith of Christ. Also, the reason the majority of mankind has not appropriated the glorious everlasting life benefits of the finished work of the cross by Christ is that the devil has blinded their spiritual eyes of understanding (11 Corinthians 4:3-4). This is done in such a way that they are not able to understand that their justification and qualification before God is a product of the faith which the root and pillar is Jesus Christ. This is clearly seen in Galatians 2:16 (KJV):

"Knowing that a man is not justified by the works of the law, but by the faith of Jesus Christ, even we have believed in Jesus Christ, that we might be justified by the faith of Christ, and not by the works of the law: for by the works of the law shall no flesh be justified." Beloved, imagine the numerous religion abounding on earth through which millions seek relationship with the Almighty God without Jesus Christ. Such fruitless and frustrating religious activities which result in uncontrollable global violence, in some cases, only can be avoided by faith in Christ. The previous scripture supports the claim Jesus made in John 14:6 (KJV), where He said: "...*I am the way, the truth, and the life: no man cometh unto the Father, but by me.*"

Without Jesus Christ (the way), insurmountable concrete road block lies between God and man. Without Christ (the truth), man is buried in the avalanche of relentless satanic assault of deception (ocean of lies). And without Christ (the life), man will for ever groan in the bottomless and horrible pit of everlasting spiritual death (separation from God for eternity).

It follows that the only entrance to the household of God Almighty is Jesus His son. And the faith that downloads these precious promises of God is faith which its root and pillar is Jesus Christ (the faith of Christ). In John 14:1 (KJV), Jesus cautioned:

"Let not your heart be troubled: ye believe in God, believe also in me."

In other words, God and Christ constitutes the roots and pillars of our belief (faith) system. This is a supernatural faith that overcomes the world and renders impossibilities possible (I John 5:4; Mark 9:23).

Will you hasten and take advantage of this precious eternal

relationship with the Omnipotent Savior (Christ), if you have not? The faith of Christ is knocking on the door of your heart. This faith is incorruptible and void of disappointment. It is a highway to everlasting peace and rest in God.

CHAPTER 13
THE HOLY SPIRIT - THE ROOT AND PILLAR OF OUR FAITH

The Bible teaches that the word of God is the word of faith, and that the word of God is also the truth (Romans 10:8; John 17:17). But the Holy Spirit is the spirit of truth (John 15:26; 16:13). If the Holy Spirit is the spirit of truth, which is the word of God; then He (the Holy Spirit) is the spirit of faith. This is a powerful truth of the gospel of the kingdom of God. Take a look at this:

"We having the same spirit of faith, according as it is written, I believed, and therefore have I spoken; we also believe, and therefore speak." (11 Corinthians 4:13 KJV)

We will discuss this scripture later in details. The Spirit referred to in this scripture is the Holy Spirit. Clearly, the Holy Spirit is the spirit of faith. Jesus gave us a very powerful revelation in the book of John 6:63, when He declared: *"It is the Spirit that quickeneth; the flesh profited nothing; the words that I speak unto you, they are Spirit and they are life."*

In other words, the Spirit gives life, while the flesh offers nothing. But the word is a container of the spirit and the life of God. Since faith comes by hearing the word and the word is Spirit, therefore, the Holy Spirit is the Spirit of faith mentioned in 11Corinthians 4;13 above.

The Holy Spirit is also the sole custodian and distributor of God's kind of faith described as the spiritual gift of faith in the Bible. This revelatory truth we see confirmed in 1 Corinthians 12:1, 8, 9a quoted below:

"Now concerning spiritual gifts, brethren, I would not have you ignorant.

For to one is given by the Spirit the word of wisdom; to another the word of knowledge by the same Spirit:

To another faith by the same Spirit;"

Faith, which is listed above as one of the nine gifts of the Holy Spirit, is administered exclusively by the Holy Spirit.

The Holy Spirit distributes and administers this gift of faith strictly by His volition. Though we are persuasively encouraged to covet it, the gift operates independent of our efforts.

Also, the Holy Spirit, in union with the regenerated (born again) human spirit of a man, produces one of the nine fruit of the spirit called faith. This is recorded in Galatians chapter 5, verse 22-23 (KJV):

"But the fruit of the Spirit is love, joy, peace, longsuffering, gentleness, goodness, faith,

meekness, temperance: against such there is no law."

Actually, our spirit man is the one that produces this fruit of faith because Jesus explained that He is the vine, and we are the branches.

"I am the vine, ye are the branches: He that abideth in me, and I in him, the same bringeth forth much fruit: for without me ye can do nothing." (John 15:5 KJV).

Evidently, it is crystal clear that the branch bears the fruit and not the vine, though the vine is the source of life. However, our spirit man that bears this fruit of faith cannot be separated from the Holy Spirit because the Bible explains in

1 Corinthians 6:17 (KJV) that they are both united. *"But he that is joined unto the Lord is one spirit."*

Indeed, our regenerated spirit is united with the Holy Spirit. Ephesians 1:13 (KJV) also confirms the union of our born again spirit with the Holy Spirit:

"In whom you also trusted, after that you heard the word of truth, the gospel of your salvation: in whom also after that ye believed, ye were sealed with that holy Spirit of promise."

We know that we are tripartite beings of spirit, soul, and body (I Thessalonians 5:23). And only our spirit can be sealed with the Holy Spirit since our soul and our body are not yet saved (James 1:21; Hebrews 10:39; Romans 8:10, 23).

"Wherefore lay apart all filtiness and superfluity of naughtiness, and received with meekness the engrafted word, which is able to save your souls."(James1:21).

"But we are not of them that draw back unto perdition; but of them that believe to the saving of the soul."(Hebrews10:39).

"And if Christ be in you, the body is dead because of sin; but the Spirit is life because of righteousness"(Romans8:10).

"And not only they, but ourselves also, which have the firstfruits of the Spirit, even we ourselves groan within ourselves, waiting for the adoption, to wit, the redemption of our body" (Romans 8:23).

The engrafted word which is able to save our soul! But of them that believe to the saving of the soul! The body is dead because of sin!

To wit, the redemption of our body!

And the Spirit is life because of righteousness!

We are tripartite beings of spirit, soul, and body (1 Thessalonians 5:23).

All these scriptures teach that only our spirit is born again and has life because of righteousness. Our soul and our body are still dead in trespasses and sins (Ephesians 2:1), awaiting salvation and glorious body replacement respectively. As a result, only our Spirit Man is united and sealed with the Holy Spirit of promise (Ephesians1:13); and bears the fruit of the spirit called faith with the help of the Holy Spirit. (Galatians 5:22).

As mentioned above, we are yet to receive our glorious bodies at the second coming of Christ (Romans 8:10, 23). Just as we are one with Christ (Hebrews 2:11), the Holy Spirit of God is also one with our born again spirit man. In fact, the Bible records that the Holy Spirit bears witness with our spirit that we are the children of God (Romans 8:16).

It's interesting to note that at the point of our regeneration, a spiritual union took place between the Holy Spirit and our born again spirit (Titus 3:4-6; I Corinthians 6:17)

II Corinthians 4:13 (KJV) exposes another dimension of the role of the Holy Spirit in our spiritual life of faith:

"We having the same Spirit of Faith, according as it is written, I believed, and therefore have I spoken; we also believe, and therefore speak."

This follows that the Holy Spirit, working with our regenerated Spirit Man (Human Spirit) is the root and pillar of the gift of faith (Ephesians 2:8, 9), the measure of faith (Romans 12:3), the victory of faith (I John 5:4), and the preciousness of faith (II Peter 1:1); all received at the point of our redemption. Wow! To God is the glory. What a generous mighty God we serve. We are loaded.

We should not forget that our redemption process was by the washing of regeneration, and renewing of the Holy Spirit (Titus 3:5).

Actually, our spirit man is the one that produces this fruit of faith because Jesus explained that He is the vine, and we are the branches.

"But after that the kindness and love of God our Saviour toward man appeared, Not by works of righteousness which we have done, but according to His mercy he saved us, by the washing of regeneration, and renewing of the Holy Ghost." (Titus 3:4,5).

No believer can live an unconscious life of the Holy Spirit and expect to experience an effective lifestyle of faith. The most important practical Christianity lesson, embedded in this section is that no believer can successfully and victoriously experience a triumphant life of faith independent of the Holy Spirit. This is true because the Holy Spirit together with the Father and the Word (Son) remain the single root and pillar of our faith. This is equivalent to the supernatural parliamentary procedure that preceded the creation of man. Here and then God requested, saying:

"......Let us (Godhead) make man in our image, after our likeness: and let them have dominion over the fish of the sea, and over the fowl of the air, and over the cattle, and over all the earth, and over every creeping thing that creepeth upon the earth." (Genesis 1:26 KJV)

No believer can live an unconscious life of the Holy Spirit and expect to experience an effective lifestyle of faith.

The Godhead - the Father, the Word, and the Holy Spirit are the three that bear record in Heaven and they are one (1 John 5:7). Any operation of faith independent of the Godhead is faithless by nature.

Also, the Holy Spirit has the supernatural mandate to ensure the effectiveness of the faith of Christ, which we practice (John 14:26).

CHAPTER 14

THE WORD OF GOD - THE ROOT AND PILLAR OF OUR FAITH

I t is impossible to separate faith from the word of God. The word of God is the distinctive feature between the faith of God and human natural faith. While the operation of the faith of God (Colossians 2:12) is completely dependent upon the word of God, human natural faith is dependent upon man's effort, available resources and the senses.

The Bible defines the word of God as the word of faith (Romans 10:8). Faith can easily be substituted for the word of God. For instance, where the Bible says in 11 Corinthians 5:7 (KJV), *"For we walk by faith, not by sight"*. We can safely say without being accused of committing error that: *"for we walk by the word of God, not by sight."*

Furthermore, we can as well peruse these statements in details in Romans 10:8 (KJV):

"But what saith it? The word is nigh thee, even in thy mouth, and in thy heart: that is, the word of faith, which we preach."

The word of God is indeed the word of faith. The Bible also declares that:

"Through faith we understand that the worlds were framed by the word of God, so that things which are seen were not made of things which do appear." (Hebrews 11:3 KJV).

It's very interesting and exciting to know and to note that the God of faith framed the world by His word of faith. This indicated that the world was made from things that were non-existent in the visible (physical) realm of existence. In other words, the world is the product of the word of God which has dynamic creative power and is also called the word of faith (Romans 8:10). Recall that in John 1:1, 14 (KJV) we read that the Word that was with God was God and was made flesh, and dwelt among us, and we beheld His glory as of the only begotten of the father, *"...full of grace and truth."*

We can conclusively confirm that like God and Jesus, the word of God is also a root and pillar of faith. Absence of faith is directly proportional to absence of the word of God. Hence, it's written:

"So then faith cometh by hearing, and hearing by the word of God." (Romans 10:17 KJV)

It is very common for believers to complain that they're suffering from lack of faith. The truth is that they are void of the word of God. They should go for the word- studying to show thyself approved of God (11Timothy2:15).

In the light of this revelatory discourse, there is therefore no doubt that without the word of God, there will be no faith; faith is the product of the word of God. Please, don't forget that our discussion is focused on God's kind of faith - the faith of the operation of God (Colossians 2:12). This category of faith is also called the faith of Jesus Christ (Galatians 2:16, 20). This is a supernatural faith which produces supernatural signs and wonders (Galatians 3:5) using the word of God as its object.

"He therefore that ministereth to you the Spirit, and worketh miracles among you, doeth he it by the works of the law, or by the HEARING OF FAITH?" (Galatians 3; 5).

As mentioned earlier, the faith of God is completely dependent on the word of God as the object and does not consider senses and the knowledge of the over-whelmed and visible antagonistic circumstances. Have you ever asked people, "Do you have faith that God will heal you?" For sure, many will respond in the affirmative. Then request that they show you the evidence of their faith. Most of the time the answer will be, "Well, I just believe that God will heal me."

The truth is that they are not confessing faith. All they have is mental hope. Faith is the substance of our hopeful expectation and the evidence of our unseen reality. This substance and evidence is the incorruptible seed which is the word of God, the word of faith,"*...and the word of grace, which is able to build you up and give you an inheritance among all them which are sanctified."* (Acts 20:32).

This explains why many believers in Christ stagger on the promises of God due to unbelief (faithlessness): because they possess not the relevant evidence of the word. They are simply and ignorantly functioning in the dangerous realm of unbelief. The Bible proved this scenario beyond reasonable doubt when it declared:

"But with whom was he (God) *grieved forty years? was it not with them that had sinned, whose carcases fell in the wilderness?*

And to whom sware he that they should not enter into his rest, but to them that believed not?

So we see that they could not enter in because of unbelief." (Hebrews 3:17-19 KJV)

"Let us therefore fear, lest, a promise being left us of entering into his rest, any of you should seem to come short of it.

For unto us was the gospel preached, as well as unto them: but the word preached did not profit them, not being mixed with faith in them that heard it." (Hebrews 4:1-2 KJV)

Now, it's obvious that the incorruptible seed of the word of God, not mixed with faith becomes fruitless. And faith without the word of God as its root and pillar produces unbelief. Effective faith that is void of unbelief and moves mountains is rooted, grounded, and reinforced by the word of God. Therefore the word of God is a supernatural root and pillar of our faith. No word from God, no reliable productive faith.

Now, it's obvious that the incorruptible seed of the word of God, not mixed with faith becomes fruitless.

CHAPTER 15
LOVE - THE ROOT AND PILLAR OF OUR FAITH

"**F**or in Jesus Christ neither circumcision availeth any thing, nor uncircumcision; but faith which worketh by love" (Galathians5:6).

The walk of faith becomes fruitless without love. Of course, this refers to the love of God - the agape love (unconditional love). Prophet Jeremiah, under the inspiration of the Holy Spirit, described the love of God saying:

"The Lord hath appeared of old unto me, saying, Yea, I have loved thee with an everlasting love: therefore with loving-kindness have I drawn thee." (Jeremiah 31:3 KJV).

The love of God is not only unconditional, but everlasting and full of the kindness of God. Also, the Bible describing the unlimited abundance of the love of God as a volumetric entity cautioned that this love is beyond human knowledge and comprehension (Ephesians 3:19).

"That Christ may dwell in your hearts by faith, that ye, being

rooted and grounded in love, May be able to comprehend with all saints what is the breadth, and length, and depth, and height; And to know the love of Christ, which passeth knowledge, that ye might be filled with all the fulness of God." (Ephesians3:17-19)

The Bible also says that God is love (I John 4:8). Now, because God is love, the love of God is a spirit and a mystery like God. I think that was what Paul was conveying in Ephesians 3:17-19. In this scripture we (believers) are also strongly encouraged to be rooted and grounded in this love of God. (Ephesians 3:17).

Why must believers be rooted and grounded in the love of God? Because our faith, which is a vital portion of our relationship with God and the foundation of our lifestyle on earth is grossly ineffective without the love of God.

"For in Jesus Christ neither circumcision availeth anything, nor uncircumcision; but faith which worketh by love." (Galatians 5:6 KJV)

"But faith which worketh by Love". If faith works by love, according to the divine statute (will), agenda, plans and purpose of God, as revealed in the holy scriptures; it follows that without love, faith will be dormant or impotent (awaiting activation). This implies that the manifestation of faith is grossly dependent on Love. No Love, no faith. Again this strongly refers to the Love of God which passes sense knowledge. The love of man at best does not measure to the level of agape (unconditional) love of God, which surpasses human comprehension.

The love of God obtained such a high level of indispensable factor in the efficacy of faith because God is love. This explains why God's kind of faith is failure proof.

Therefore the word of God is a supernatural root and pillar of our faith. No word from God, no reliable productive faith.

Unfortunately, many believers are yet to comprehend the truth that faith is completely dependent upon the love of God and not upon the love of man or Law of Moses. That explains why so many people are still struggling in the realm of a productive lifestyle of faith. Faith *"worketh by love."* Without love, faith ceases to work. What love? The answer mentioned earlier is the love of God - the agape love (unconditional love).

This Love of God (Agape) is not elusive to us (believers). In fact, the Bible says it's poured out in our hearts by the Holy Spirit (Romans5:5). But God, realizing that we lack the capacity to produce this kind of Love; imparts it in our human spirit (heart) as a gift, just like our righteousness. This, we must understand in order to practice effectual faith (Philemon 6). By this, I mean that, knowledge of the relationship between faith and love; and foreknowledge of the fact that this love is at our disposal, empowers us to release our faith without doubt.

"For God so loved the world, that He gave His only begotten Son; that whosoever believeth in Him should not perish, but have everlasting life" (John3:16).

The book of John 3:16 teaches that the love of God expressed through Christ is capable of delivering and protecting man from everlasting destruction and death. This explains how powerful the love of God is, but its benefits are only for those who believe (capable of exercising their faith, as stated below):

"But we are bound to give thanks always to God for you, brethren beloved of the Lord, because God hath from the beginning chosen you to salvation through sanctification of the Spirit and belief of the truth." (11 Thessalonians 2:13 KJV).

"Belief of the truth". For sure, you must believe. You must exercise your faith.

1. Thomas Nelson once defined the love of God as "God's absolute and unqualified goodwill." But the love of God is not only unconditional, unearned, unmerited, undeserved; but also a container of the power of God. In comparison, the horizontal dimension of love, which is man's natural love for God, humanity and himself; is very much limited and selfish? To the surprise of many, man's natural love is a hindrance to the effectiveness of our faith because it is of the flesh (void of power). Again, faith works effectively by the love of God (Galatians 5:6). Faith cannot be separated from the love of God as can be seen below:

"But ye, brethren, are not in darkness: that that day should overtake you as a thief.

Ye are all the children of light, and the children of the day: we are not of the night, nor of darkness.

Therefore let us not sleep, as do others; but let us watch and be sober."

"But let us, who are of the day, be sober, putting on the

breastplate of faith and love; and for an helmet, the hope of salvation." (I Thessalonians 5:4-6, 8 KJV)... "breastplate of faith and love"

Without ambiguity the above scriptures teach that faith, as a spiritual defensive weapon and armor, needs the supporting pillar of love. Again this refers to the unlimited powerful love of God. My question in the above context is this: are believers lacking in this supernatural love of God that has the power to energize and perfect our faith? The answer is: absolutely not, as stated previously.

Faith "worketh by love." Without love, faith ceases to work.

God who commanded His righteous ones to live by His faith knowing that this faith is also ineffective without His love; in His own infinite kindness and mercy, saturated our heart (regenerated human spirit) with His agape love.

"And this hope will not lead to disappointment. For we know how dearly God loves us, because He has given us the Holy Spirit to fill our hearts with his love." (Romans 5:5 NLT)

Please note that before God filled us with His love which is designed to strengthen our faith among other roles; He first of all commanded (demonstrated) this love towards us.

"But God commanded his love toward us, in that, while we were yet sinners, Christ died for us." (Romans 5:8).

Incidentally, we are not only the products of this miraculous love of God, but also the beneficiaries, custodians, and distributors. Following this, He (God) commanded us to be rooted and grounded in His love. He also exhorts us not to exercise this love in hypocrisy.

"Let love be without dissimulation. Abhor that which is evil; cleave to that which is good" (Romans 12:9).

The capacity and role of the Love of God in our daily labor of faith must be approached with seriousness.

Again you cannot separate faith from love. Many believers are experiencing spiritual fatalities in their lifestyle of faith because of conspicuous absence of the knowledge of love as a spiritual pillar of faith.

Recall that our focus is on God's kind of faith. That is, faith of the operation of God (Colossians 2:12) - the faith that is operated by Christ who is in us; the hope of glory. Is it right for us to assume that Christ can operate the faith of God in our lives without the love of God?

While releasing your faith in the presence of any offensive and challenging situation, you must be conscious of the truth that God's love for you supersedes your challenges and the fruitlessness of your faith. It's also a mighty pillar supporting your faith. Therefore, you should practice your faith, void of doubt, with gross assurance of success.

Faith is a possibility in our lives:

1. Because God is love (1 John 4:8).
2. And this love of God is poured out in our hearts (Romans 5:5).

3. And Christ is operating the faith of God in us (Colossians 2:12; Galatians 2:16, 20).

And this faith works by the love of God.

As the righteous, new creation, children of God, instructed and mandated to live by faith; knowledge, understanding, wisdom, and consciousness of the truth that love is a spiritual supportive pillar of vitality and productivity in our lifestyle of faith cannot be over emphasized. How do we practically factor in love in our daily work of faith?

First and foremost we must realize that our faith remains unproductive without love (Galatians 5:6). Secondly, we must understand that the love in question is the love of God for us which is poured out in our heart and it is our subsequent responsibility to express this love to God, our neighbors and ourselves.

"Be ye therefore followers of God, as dear children; And walk in love, as Christ also hath loved us, and hath given himself for us an offering and a sacrifice to God for a sweet smelling savour." (Ephesians5:1, 2).

Also, deep rooted knowledge of God's love for us precipitates unshakable assurance that God is able to honor our faith in Him and also deliver His promises to us. Hence, the Holy Spirit, through Apostle Paul said:

"Having therefore, brethren, boldness to enter into the holiest by the blood of Jesus, By a new and living way, which he hath consecrated for us, through the veil, that is to say, his flesh; And having a high priest over the house of God; Let us draw near with a true heart in FULL ASSURANCE of FAITH, having our

hearts sprinkled from an evil conscience, (doubtful heart) *and our bodies washed with pure water* (our flesh and senses denied through practice-Hebrew5:14). *Let us HOLD FAST the profession* (confession) *of our FAITH without wavering; for he is FAITHFUL that promised*" (Hebrew10:19-23).

Finally, we must be rooted and grounded in the love of God (Ephesians3:17). One of the dimensions of being rooted and grounded in the love of God is to allow the Holy Spirit to enable us to understand the length, width, height, and the depth of the love of God. According to the Bible, this knowledge surpasses human comprehension (Ephesians 3:18-19). In other words, the love of God for the new creation is not only a mystery but possesses a limitless dimension (volume) and magnitude to enable us function in the fullness of God as Jesus did in His earthly ministry (Ephesians 3:19; John 14:12).

Incidentally, we are not only the products of this miraculous love of God, but also the beneficiaries, custodians, and distributors.

How does this apply to our faith? The implication and application of this love, and its knowledge to our faith is that the love of God for us is so great that our simple faith and trust in Him and His promises are of great value. It breaks the power of unbelief and impossibility in our lives and provokes divine intervention when we launch our faith against challenging and adverse life circumstances.

In the book of 11 Kings 6, Prophet Elisha applied the above

principle of faith against the military siege of the Syrian Army. When he prayed and made a confession of faith and said: "*they that be with us are more than they that be with them;*" God not only besieged the territory with massive heavenly horses and chariots of fire; but He also granted Elisha's servant a supernatural insight into the realm of the spirit. May God grant us supernatural eyesight to enable us consistently exercise spiritual insight in this end time.

Recall that the Jews in the wilderness failed and could not enter into the rest of God because they refused to mix the word of God with faith (Hebrews 4:2). Therefore when you - as the new creation release your faith, remember that God rewards those who diligently trust Him and His promises according to His unconditional love.

Honestly, I cannot find the appropriate words and sentences to express the truth that God is more interested than us in seeing us (believers) appropriate the benefits of the cross which He had already freely provided for us through His grace (Romans 8:32; 1 Corinthians 2:12).

Our challenge and failure to appropriate God's benefits is in the realm of faith. Yet His word tells us: "...*My grace is sufficient for thee: for my strength is made perfect in weakness.*" (II Corinthians 12:9).

"*And God is able to make all grace abound towards you; that ye, always having all sufficiency in all things, may abound to every good works.*" (11 Corinthians 9:8 KJV).

How can one adequately explain the above scripture? Just suffice it to say that the new creation is obligated to produce unlimited good work; out of the abundance and sufficiency of resources, freely given to him by the grace of God. But, don't forget that faith is a requirement. This next scripture is also helpful:

"For ye know the grace of our Lord Jesus Christ, that, though he was rich, yet for your sakes he became poor, that ye through his poverty might be rich." (11 Corinthians 8:9 KJV)

Here the power of lack and poverty is broken over the life of the new creation as a result of the grace of our Lord Jesus Christ and faith in God who is Love.

"For if by one man's offence death reigned by one; much more they which receive abundance of grace and of the gift of righteousness shall reign in life by one, Jesus Christ." (Romans 5:17 KJV)

We joyfully observe that every believer is authorized to exercise dominion and ruler-ship in life as a result of the abundance of grace and the gift of righteousness lavished on us in our new birth.

"What shall we then say to these things? If God be for us, who can be against us?

He that spared not his own Son, but delivered him up for us all, how shall he not with him also freely give us all things?" (Romans 8:31-32 KJV)

Wait a minute! What about the revelation of the spirit we have received in I Corinthians 2:12 (KJV)?

"Now we have received, not the spirit of the world, but the spirit which is of God; that we might know the things that are freely given to us of God."

We can now see why God demands that we must live by faith - because He has freely given us all things by grace.

From the previous scriptures, I conclude that there are two things we should not petition God for. These are:

(i) what He had already freely given to us - all spiritual blessings in heavenly places in Christ and all things that pertain unto life and godliness (Ephesians 1:3; 11 Peter 1:3); and

(ii) what He had authorized us to execute. For instance:

"And these signs shall follow them that believe; In my name shall they cast out devils; they shall speak with new tongues;

They shall take up serpents: and if they drink any deadly thing it shall not hurt them; they shall lay hands on the sick, and they shall recover." (Mark 16:17-18 KJV)

For what God had commanded you to do, please don't hesitate to exercise your authority. But for what He had already given you, go to Him with thanksgiving and celebrate in advance the manifestation of your expectation. Also, don't forget that the activation and performance of the faith of Christ during His earthly ministry was at its peak not because of His deity or perfection but because of His love and compassion for the oppressed. For it is written:

"And Jesus went forth, and saw a great multitude, and was moved with compassion toward them, and he healed their sick." (Matthew 14:14 KJV)

"How God anointed Jesus of Nazareth with the Holy Ghost and with power: who went about doing good, and healing all that were oppressed of the devil; for God was with him." (Acts 10:38 KJV)

We (the new creation) too, can maximize our faith and corresponding results by mixing our faith with the love of God which is poured lavishly in our hearts by the Holy Spirit (Romans 5:5).

Our challenge and failure to appropriate God's benefits is in the realm of faith.

CHAPTER 16
PATIENCE - PILLAR OF OUR FAITH

No doubt, patience is the panacea for weak and unproductive faith. It also has the power to eradicate doubt, unbelief, and the stronghold of senses. These are all enemies of faith. Many murmur and complain of lack of or weak faith, while in reality the corresponding challenging factor is the absence of patience in their faith life. If we're conscious of patience in the process of releasing our faith in a particular situation; there will be no room for doubt and unbelief.

Every believer is authorized to exercise dominion and ruler-ship in life as a result of the abundance of grace and the gift of righteousness lavished on us in our new birth.

In other words, whenever we launch our faith, targeting a

particular unseen reality, if we did not experience instantaneous breakthrough, then patience becomes the weapon to deploy in order to pull down the potential strongholds of doubt, unbelief, and the senses. Jesus dealt with this issue in the case of the epileptic young lad (Mark 9:14-29; Matthew 17:14-21). After rebuking the demon, the lad fell down, and seemed to have died, but Jesus patiently lifted him up. This was unlike the disciples who withdrew when the boy fell down. Satan and his demons simply and successfully deceived the disciples through sense knowledge. I must add here that sense knowledge, doubt and lack of knowledge of the word of God are the greatest enemies of faith.

What is patience?

Patience is the ability to bear afflictions without anxiety, murmuring and crumbling. Synonyms of patience are long suffering, determination, endurance, tolerance, and perseverance among many others. Obviously many who become needless casualties of the relentless assault of doubt, unbelief, and senses are those who intentionally or inadvertently refuse to consider patience or any of those synonyms in the realm of faith.

So far, these emphases on the relationship between patience, faith on one hand and doubt, unbelief, and senses on the other hand is necessary because of the tremendous rate of failure among faith practitioners. The Bible records that patience is the nature of God.

"Now the God of patience and consolation grant you to be likeminded one towards another according to Christ Jesus." (Romans 15:5 KJV).

Accordingly God is a God of patience. And because we're partakers of the divine nature of God, we too are partakers of the spiritual patience of God. This is confirmed in Galatians 5:22-23, which lists patience (long suffering) as one of the "fruit" of our spirit. But of paramount importance is the fact that patience cannot be separated from faith. For sure, patience is one of the pillars of faith. Experientially, in most cases where faith seemed to have failed, advent and infusion of patience have always resulted in the resurrection and productivity of faith.

Many believers murmur and complain of lack of or weak faith, while in reality the corresponding challenging factor is the absence of patience in their faith life.

<u>*Application of Patience:*</u> In the Epistles, numerous verses exist, which underscore the importance and inevitability of patience in the efficacy of faith. In this context we will be able to examine but a few:

1. *"But if we hope for that we see not, then do we with patience wait for it."* (Romans 8:25 KJV)

Recall that hope is a partaker of faith according to Hebrews 11:1a KJV - *"Now faith is the substance of things hoped for."*

Romans 8:25 simply explains that because hope is a factor in our walk of faith, patience therefore becomes vitally important as to the actualization and realization of our hopeful expectation.

"But if we hope for that we see not, then do we with patience wait for it."(Romans 8:25). This is true because faith deals with the unseen but realities of God in His Grace. Hence patience is the

most powerful force required to provoke the manifestation of every unseen reality.

2. *"**We are bound to thank God always for you, brethren, as it is meet, because that your faith growth exceedingly, and the charity of everyone of you all toward each other aboundeth;***

So that we ourselves glory in you in the churches of God for your <u>patience and faith</u> in all your persecutions and tribulations that ye endure."* (II Thessalonians 1:3-4 KJV)

It becomes very clear that patience plays a very important role in the growth of faith and the application of faith to overcome persecutions and tribulations. We see this in 1 John 5:4, where the scripture clearly informed us that, "*whatsoever is born of God overcometh the world and this is the victory that overcometh the world, even our faith*". By this, I understand that God has given us the gift of victory, which is to be activated by our faith to overcome persecutions and tribulations of this world. But 11Thessalonians 1: 3-4, above, added that patience is needed as a reinforcement for faith against persecutions and tribulations.

3. "*Wherefore seeing we also are compassed about with so great a cloud of witnesses, let us lay aside every weight, and the sin which doth so easily beset us, and let us run with patience the race that is set before us,*

Looking unto Jesus the author and finisher of our faith." (Hebrews 12:1-2a KJV).

Apparently, successful application of the faith of Jesus Christ in our earthly struggles and life of faith demands a tremendous amount of patience. Lack of patience, not only hinders the effectiveness of our faith, but also tends to draw us away from

Christ who is the Author and Finisher of our faith and have us focus on the circumstance.

Hence patience is the most powerful force required to provoke the manifestation of every unseen reality.

We all know that this is the agenda of Satan and his cohorts (the world and the flesh).

Faith, Patience and the Promises of God:

The Bible makes it very clear that God Himself qualified us to become partakers of His everlasting inheritance (Colossians 1:12; Hebrews 9:15). Secondly, because the inheritance or promises are made available to us by the grace of God, faith is required as the instrument of appropriation (Romans 4:16). But why are so many believers still struggling in their ability to experience the manifestation of the promises of God, irrespective of the fact that many have consciously grown in their knowledge and application of faith? No doubt the answer is the absence of patience at times; especially when we are confronted with conspicuous time lag.

Please note that patience emerges as a vital factor in the manifestation of our promises, despite the presence of faith, simply because of the interference of time lag. Consider the case of healing! The Bible in one instance declares:

"He (God) *sent his word, and healed them, and delivered them from their destructions."* (Psalm 107:20 KJV)

"Who (Christ) *his own self bare our sins in his own body on the tree that we, being dead to sins, should live unto righteousness: by whose stripes ye were healed."* (I Peter 2:24 KJV).

These promises are done deals because they are in the past. They were spiritually ordained and accomplished before the world began; but physically executed on the cross by Christ. Check out this:

"Who (God) *hath saved* (Sozo - including healing, deliverance, wholeness, soundness, prosperity, protection and preservation) *us, and called us with an holy calling, not according to our works, but according to his own purpose and grace, which was given us in Christ Jesus BEFORE THE WORLD BEGAN. But is now made manifest by the appearing of our Saviour Jesus Christ, who hath abolished death, and hath brought life and immortality to light,"* (11Timothy1:9, 10).

It's glorious to note that all the promises of God for us are done deals in Christ.

If the healings of Psalm 107:20 and 1 Peter 2:24 manifest instantaneously, that is termed miraculous healings which may occur as a result of the application of faith in God and His promises. Another category of healing is what the Bible calls recovery as recorded in Mark 16:17-18 (KJV).

"And these signs shall follow them that believe (faith); In my name shall they cast out devils; they shall speak with new tongues;

They shall take up serpents; and if they drink any deadly thing, it shall not hurt them; they shall lay hands on the sick and they shall recover."

"And they shall recover." Obviously, in this context, recovery is not only the product of faith, but also of patience. For some people, tremendous amount (heavy dosage) of patience is required. Please remember as a new creation in Christ, your spirit is a bearer of unlimited patience (Galatians 5:22-23). Our heavenly father cannot demand from us what He has not provided for us by His grace (II Corinthians 9:8; 8:9; 12:9).

The importance of patience in successful and fruitful application of our faith in challenging situations and in obtaining the promises of God is also explained by the following scriptures:

"That ye be not slothful, but followers of them who through faith and patience inherit the promises".

And so, after he (Abraham) *had patiently endured, he obtained the promise."* (Hebrews 6:12, 15 KJV)

"Cast not away therefore your confidence (faith), *which hath great recompence of reward.*

For ye have need of patience, that, after ye have done the will of God, ye might receive that promise.

Now the just shall live by faith:" (Hebrews 10:35-36, 38a KJV)

Clearly stated, patience is a companion of faith.

In all the scriptures above, patience positions itself as a pillar of super structure in the successful and fruitful execution of faith. It's of supernatural significance to note that as you patiently superimpose patience in your faith life, your faith in turn reinforces the supply of patience to your battle of faith as we see succinctly explained in James 1:2-3 (KJV):

"My brethren, count it all joy when ye fall into divers temptations;

Knowing this, that the trying of your faith worketh patience."

This simply means that our trials are also designed to supply us with patience. So, patience has a double standard of sourcing.

Indeed patience is a stronghold of faith. While faith is indispensable in reinforcing a stronghold of patience. The next time you intend to release your faith, remember your stronghold of patience in case there is unexpected interference of delay or time lapse. The ball is in your court and your court is your realm of dominion by faith.

It's glorious to note that all the promises of God for us are done deals in Christ.

In considering patience as an important element of faith, we must learn a big lesson from our father Abraham. In the absence of enduring patience, Abraham and Sarah bargained for Ishmael and the disastrous consequences are still sweeping across the globe. By the grace of God, Abraham recovered from that tragedy and the Bible, encouraging every student of faith said the following:

"And being not weak in faith, he (Abraham) considered not his own body now dead, when he was about hundred years old, neither yet the deadness of Sarah's womb. He staggered not at the promises of God through unbelief; but was strong in faith

giving glory to God. And been fully persuaded that, what He had promised, He was able also to perform." (Romans 4: 19-21).

Indeed, unbelief, which is a chronic enemy of faith, is a product of impatience. Patience therefore becomes an inevitable element of faith in the absence of miracles. Every successful student of faith, practices the mindset and consciousness of patience.

Our trials are also designed to supply us with patience. So, patience has a double standard of sourcing.

CHAPTER 17
PRAYER - PILLAR OF OUR FAITH

No doubt there is an inevitable connection between faith and prayer as we are commanded in Matthew 17:20 to authoritatively say unto this mountain to be removed. For sure, speaking to the challenging mountains of life by faith is authoritative prayer. In other words, authoritative prayer in this instance is the logistics that convey our bullets of faith to our targets. *"If you have faith as a grain of mustard seed, ye shall say...."* We all know that seed also refers to the words of God.

Prayer is a supernatural carrier (logistics) of faith.

Simply conveyed, authoritative prayer of the word, like a rocket launcher, propels your faith to your target. Without prayer, your faith remains in a state of inertia. Your mission of faith becomes mission impossible. Dynamic faith is a product of authoritative prayer. The woman with the issue of blood authoritatively declared, *"If I may but touch his garment, I shall be whole."* (Matthew 9:21 KJV). And when she did and was made whole, Jesus said, "....*Daughter, be of good comfort; thy faith hath made thee whole......*" (Matthew 9:22 KJV).

Also when blind Bartimaeus (the son of Timaeus) addressed Jesus saying,

"Thou son of David, have mercy upon me.

Lord, that I might receive my sight.

And Jesus said unto him, Go thy way; thy faith hath made thee whole. And immediately he received his sight and followed Jesus in the way." (Mark 10: 48c, 51c, 52 KJV).

Amazingly Jesus Himself confirmed in that passage that authoritative prayer is a carrier of faith. Apostle James in his letters also explained:

"If any of you lack wisdom, let him ask of God, that giveth to all men liberally, and upbraideth not; and it shall be given him.

But let him ask in faith, nothing wavering. For he that wavereth is like a wave of the sea driven with the wind and tossed." (James 1:5-6 KJV)

Let him ask in faith. Prayer is a supernatural carrier (logistics) of faith.

"Is any among you afflicted? let him pray.

And the prayer of faith shall save the sick." (James 5:13a, 15a KJV)

Again, prayer stands as the pillar of faith. Both faith and prayer are inseparable. One can clearly see in the scripture above that, faith is a container of prayer. This, partially provides reason for unanswered prayers. Authentic and effective prayer, as recorded above, must be a prayer of faith. Take a look at this tri-union combination:

"And this is the confidence (faith) that we have in Him (God), that, if we ask (prayer) any thing according to His will (word), he heareth us. And if we know that he hear us, whatsoever we ask, we know that we have the petitions that we desired of Him." (1 John 5:14, 15).

Here, we learn that, the activation of the manifestation of the promises of God; requires a supernatural combination of faith, prayer and the word of God. In other words, we're sure of answered prayers; if we faithfully pray the word of God.

Speaking to the challenging mountains of life by faith is authoritative prayer.

When next you propose to launch your faith, please do that prayerfully. Prayerful faith is a winning faith.

CHAPTER 18
CONFESSION (DECLARATION) - PILLAR OF OUR FAITH

C onfession here does not mean that relating to sin but the confession of faith. There is no faith in sin. Primarily, people commit sin because they don't have faith in God in that situation. They refuse to believe that God can rescue them from whatever is drawing them to sin and thereby drawing them away from God. Unfortunately, this simple truth is unknown to many. So, the solution to sin is faith in God. Sin is a partaker of doubt, unbelief, and faithlessness as confirmed by Romans Chapter 14:23 (KJV):

"And he that doubteth is damned if he eat, because he eateth not of faith: for whatsoever is not of faith is sin."

In another parlance, anything inconsistent with faith is sinful. However, faith itself according to the scriptures is righteousness because the scriptures say a lot about *"the righteousness which is of God by faith."* (Philippians 3:9). In the New Testament (covenant), righteousness is a product of faith. And faith is considered a righteous act. However, this righteous faith is a talking faith. It's a voice activated faith. This is confirmed by so many scriptures. Any action of faith without confession (proclamation or declaration) is tantamount to failure.

"But the righteousness which is of faith speaketh on this wise, Say not in thine heart, Who shall ascend into heaven? (that is, to bring down Christ from above:)." (Romans 10:6 KJV).

There is no faith in sin. Primarily, people commit sin because they don't have faith in God in that situation.

"Faith speaketh on this wise." Faith therefore, is a speaker. Faith adopted confession (speaking) as a factor of logistics. If faith is a rocket, then confession is a rocket launcher.

Romans 1:16-17 also confirms that the manifestation of our gift of righteousness, through the hearing of the gospel of Christ is a product of our living and dynamic faith. Therefore, faith in God is an act of righteousness to God, and righteousness is faith in God.

Romans 10:6, shows that one of the characteristics of our faith is its speaking or talking dimension. *"But the righteousness which is of faith speaketh."*

Our faith is a speaking faith, a talking faith - a faith whose principal operating system is confession or declaration. Without confession, our faith is dead, even the origin of our faith is the origin of confession because the Bible declares that our faith comes by hearing and hearing by the word of God (Romans 10:17). Without confession or declaration of the word, there will be no hearing of the word and without the hearing of the word; there will be no operation of faith. A great grand daughter of Smith Wigglesworth (one of the most powerful evangelist of humanity) once said that her great grand father always read the Bible loud because ; he is a strong believer of Romans 4:17 (Faith comes by hearing and hearing by the word of God).

Confession therefore is a pillar of faith. Many are operating dead faith because of the absence of confession in their strategy and methodology of operation of faith. Productive faith is a product of the confession or declaration of the relevant word of God.

David had faith in the name of the Lord as a spiritual stronghold of the righteous as recorded in Proverbs 18:10 (The name of the Lord is a strong tower: the righteous runneth into it, and is safe).

Anything inconsistent with faith is sinful.

When in conflict with the Goliath of Gath, how did David exercise this faith? He simply confessed and proclaimed to Goliath saying:

"Thou comest to me with a sword, and with a spear, and with a shield: but I come to thee in the name of the Lord of hosts, the God of the armies of Israel, whom thou hast defied." (1 Samuel 17:45 KJV).

David did not end there. He went further and concluded by saying:

"And all this assembly shall know that the Lord saveth not with sword and spear: for the battle is the Lord's, and he will give you

into our hands. "The battle is the Lord's"; is another scripture he quoted.

"So David prevailed over the Philistine with a sling and with a stone, and smote the Philistine, and slew him; but there was no sword in the hand of David." (I Samuel 17:47, 50 KJV).

"So there was no sword in the hand of David." Accordingly, David provoked divine intervention and miraculous spectacle, by simply confessing his faith (the word of God that he believed in his heart).

Indeed the battle of life is the battle of faith, because, *"the Lord savest not with sword and spear."* What lesson can we learn from this incident? Beloved, God does not need our assistance when we engage Him in our struggles. Nothing pleases Him but faith. *"But without faith it is impossible to please Him* (God)". (Hebrews 11:6). And, moreover; it's *"not by might, not by power, but by my spirit, saith the Lord of hosts"* (Zechariah 4:6 KJV). And the word of faith (Romans 10:8), we believe in our heart and declare with our mouth; is spirit and life (John 6:63).

So, train yourself to always believe the word and speak the word to unfriendly challenging circumstances. Then, joyfully watch them flee from you in seven different ways and fall for your sake; according to scriptures.

In 1 Chronicles 13: 9-10, Uzza had a good intention to assist God in what seemingly looked like a fall, but unfortunately for him, the result was suicidal- he was divinely electrocuted.

Faith carries so much power that you cannot take it for granted. This is simply because it derives its root from the word of God. - It is fulfilled by and in the Spirit.

And, *"The words that I speak unto you, they are spirit, and they are life."* (John 6:63).

"..And this word is the word of faith..." (Romans 10:8 KJV).

Take a look at this powerful word of promise:

"He will keep the feet of his saints, and the wicked shall be silent in darkness; for by strength shall no man prevail." (1 Samuel 2:9 KJV)

Because His word operates by the power of the Holy Spirit, therefore, by human strength shall no man prevail, but by faith and victory is inevitable. This faith and the corresponding victory come by hearing the confession of the word of God.

Productive faith is a product of the confession or declaration of the relevant word of God.

Without controversy, our battle is the battle of faith; therefore, we must fight the good fight of faith. We must earnestly contend for the faith which was once delivered unto the saints (1 Timothy 6:12; Jude 3). Like David, boldness in relentless and fearless declaration of the promises or the word of God is the divine act of faith that certainly provokes divine intervention.

This procedure is the supernatural methodology of dynamic operative and productive faith as ordained by our God of faith. Don't forget that God by confession calls those things that be not as though they were (Romans 4:17).

Faith, Victory and Declaration:

It's written: *"For whatsoever is born of God overcometh the world: and this is the victory that overcometh the world, even our faith,"* (1 John 5:4 KJV).

Every believer in Christ is the offspring of God and we are begotten of God victoriously. We're born again, recreated, and regenerated as victorious sons and daughters of the Most High God. We're products of victory. Victory is in our genes, in our blood, and in our beings - our spirit is the spirit of victory, our life is the life of victory, and our mission is that of victory, and our commission is also of victory. Our dominion of the fallen world as Christ did is also victorious by nature. We are spiritually and naturally victorious.

According to the scriptures, the source of our victory, the logistics of our victory, the weapon and the armor of our victory is our faith. And this faith is manifested by hearing the word of God, and also released or operated by confession.

Jesus following the Psalmist gave a unique, outstanding and elaborate lecture on the confession of faith. This He declared:

"For verily, I say unto you, If you have faith as a grain of mustard seed, ye shall say unto this mountain, Remove hence to yonder place; and it shall remove; and nothing shall be impossible unto you." (Matthew 17:20 KJV).

"And nothing shall be impossible unto you." So, the power of impossibility is terminated by the confession of faith-filled word of God.

Again, it's important you know that you're operating a dead faith without confession. You must open your mouth and speak in order to hear and exercise faith. The Holy Spirit of truth, through the Psalmist and before Christ invaded planet earth, also taught briefly saying: "*I believed* (faith), *therefore have I spoken: I was greatly afflicted.*" (Psalm 116:10 KJV). This was quoted by the same Holy Spirit through Apostle Paul in II Corinthians 4:13 as follows:

"We having the same spirit of faith, according as it is written, I believed, and therefore have I spoken; we also believe, and therefore speak."

I believe, and therefore speak. Amazing! Faith is an issue of the heart and of the mouth. In other words, you process the faith in your heart (spirit and soul) and you release it through your mouth by confession. Romans 10:8-10 (KJV) is a perfect lecture on the role of confession as a pillar of faith:

"But what saith it? The word is nigh thee, even in thy mouth, and in thy heart: that is, the word of faith, which we preach;

That if thou shalt confess with thy mouth the Lord Jesus, and shalt believe in thine heart that God hath raised him from the dead, thou shalt be saved.

For with the heart man believeth unto righteousness; and with the mouth confession is made unto salvation."

Briefly explained, believing the word of faith in our heart, guarantees our justification (gift of righteousness) with God, while the confession of the same word of faith with our mouth secures our deliverance (salvation).

In my ministerial experience, I've heard some people murmur and complain thus: "I've been believing and confessing, yet, I'm void of victory in my affliction or challenge."

Without controversy, our battle of the mind, is the battle of faith;
therefore, we must fight the good fight of faith.

Please, if you identify with the above situation, follow religiously (consistent and conscientious regularity), the Holy Spirit counsel in Hebrews 3:1, 2; 4:14 ISV):

"Therefore, holy brothers, partners in a heavenly calling, keep your focus on Jesus, the apostle and high priest of our confession.

He was faithful to the one who appointed him, just as Moses was in all God's household."

"Therefore, since we have a great high priest who has gone to heaven, Jesus the Son of God, let us live our lives consistent with our confession of faith."

Also Hebrews 10:23 declares, *"Let us hold fast the profession* (confession) *of our faith without wavering; (for he is faithful that promised;)"*

Remember, the moment you believe and release your faith by confession, you must relentlessly, without doubt or unbelief, maintain your confession till the arrival or, the manifestation of your expectation.

The maintenance of our confession becomes easy and effectual if we learn from Abraham who is the father of our faith.

"He staggered not at the promise of God through unbelief; but was strong in faith, giving glory to God." (Romans 4:20 KJV).

Abraham held on to his confession by *"giving glory to God."* Also, like Abraham, as recorded in Romans 4:21, we must be *"...fully persuaded that, what he had promised, he was able to perform".* Our God is a promise keeper. But don't forget to factor in the glorious praise and worship, with tenacious persuasiveness, as we patiently wait for the manifestation of our expectation.

"Faithful is he that calleth you, who also will do it." (1 Thessalonians 5:24 KJV)

Therefore the maintenance of our confession is very necessary. Approaching your giant by faith but with your mouth shut is a voluntary suicide attempt.

Many are operating dead faith because of the absence of confession in their strategy and methodology of operation of faith.

As you confront your adversaries, please learn to vehemently open your mouth wide so that God can fill it with miracles, signs and wonders that will please your heart (Psalm 81:10b).

CHAPTER 19
SOUND MIND - PILLAR OF OUR FAITH

"*T*" *he only thing that matters is that you continue to live as good citizens in a manner worthy of the gospel of the Messiah. Then, whether I come to see you or whether I stay away, I may hear all about you - that you are standing firm in one spirit, struggling with one mind for the faith of the gospel.*" (Philippians 1:27 ISV)

"Struggling with one mind for the faith of the gospel". Indeed, faith has a mind set. The mind is an inevitable element and component of the faith of the righteous. The gospel of our Lord Jesus Christ (the faith of Christ) is first received by the faculty of the mind, before the spirit man; where the process of regeneration and redemption takes place. The mind and the spirit of a man is what the Bible calls the heart of a man in some scriptures.

"*Thou wilt keep him* (the believer) *in perfect peace, whose mind is stayed* (focused) *on thee: because he trusteth* (has faith) *in thee.*" (Emphases are mine - Isaiah 26:3 KJV)

No doubt, the faith and thus, life of a believer is volatile without a sound and stable mind. The results of a sound and stable mind of faith are trust in God and manifestation of the promises of God; among which is peace.

Approaching your giant by faith but with your mouth shut is a voluntary suicide attempt.

We must understand that our spirit and soul (emotion, mind, and will) are the departments of our heart where the word of faith is planted. Unfortunately, our soul is not recreated when we become born again, and therefore must be renewed to the state of a sound mind with the word of God if we expect our faith to be effective.

Some Useful Definitions:

Actually, the Bible is not specific about the definition of the heart of a man. However, the following attempts will be helpful. Whether you agree or not, please let us not be distracted from our focus, which is the relationship between a sound mind and an effective lifestyle of faith.

1. The heart of a man in the Bible refers to the invisible innermost part of a man.
2. The invisible, innermost part of a man could be divided into two: the spirit and the soul.
3. Some believe that the spirit of a man can be divided into three:
a) Intuition - which is the organ of revelation knowledge.

b) Conscience - which is the platform of conviction of good or evil.

c) Communion - which is the platform of communication and fellowship with the spirit realm.

4. Some believe that the soul of a man is divided into three also:

a) The mind - which is the thinking faculty (seat of reasoning).

b) The will - which is the organ of volition or simply called: the decision maker.

c) Emotion - which is the house of feelings.

5. Also, the mind has the following division:

a) The Memory- which is the organ of storage of facts (the information saver).

b) Contemplation or meditation- This is the thought-processing organ.

c) Imagination - the seat of the formation of mental images and pictures. This is a very powerful organ as we all know by experience.

Of course, we (believers) all agree with 1 Thessalonians 5:23 (KJV) which divides man into three: "*And the very God of peace sanctify you wholly; and I pray God your whole spirit and soul and body be preserved blameless unto the coming of our Lord Jesus Christ.*"

In some cases, when the Bible mentions the heart of a man, it could be referring to the spirit and soul (the invisible part of a man). Sometimes, it refers to the spirit of a man only or the soul of a man only; or sometimes, it refers to the mind of a man only or the will of a man, or the emotion only.

As you confront your adversaries, please learn to vehemently open your mouth wide so that God can fill it with miracles, signs and wonders that will please your heart (Psalm 81:10b).

We must rely on the Holy Spirit to enlighten the eyes of our understanding concerning what the Bible calls the heart at any time and in any context. For instance, when Proverbs 23:7 says, *"For as he thinketh in his heart, so is he,"* we quickly infer that the organ of the mind is involved in our thinking process. So, this scripture refers to the mind as the heart of a man.

But when the Bible says, *"The heart is deceitful above all things and desperately wicked: who can know it"* (Jeremiah 17:9 KJV), it introduces another dimension to the subject matter. Talking about a believer in Christ, his spirit man who is part of his heart is regenerated (recreated), made holy, and righteous and united with the Lord Jesus Christ and the Holy Spirit (Ephesians 4:17-24; I Peter 3:3, 4; Romans 8:8-10, 22-23; 1 Corinthians 6:17).

The gospel of our Lord Jesus Christ (the faith of Christ) is first received by the faculty of the mind, before the spirit man; where the process of regeneration and redemption takes place.

As a result, our spirit cannot be wicked. Our regenerated Spirit

Man is exactly like Christ, according to scriptures (1 John 4:17). He (a believer) has the spirit of Christ (Galatians 4:6). He has the mind of Christ (1 Corinthians 2:16). He has the holiness, righteousness, and the nature of God (Ephesians 4:24; 11 Peter 1:4). He is united with Christ and the Holy Spirit (1Corinthians 6:17). In 11 Peter 3:4, the spirit of a believer is called the hidden man of the heart, ornament, meek and quiet spirit; who is incorruptible and of great price in the sight of God. In 11 Corinthians 4:16, he is the inward man that is renewed daily.

But our un-regenerated soul (mind, will, and emotion), who is also part of our heart; can be desperately wicked. In other words, for the new creation believers:

i) Half of our heart (spirit) is recreated righteous, holy and void of wickedness. He (the Spirit Man) relates, communicates and fellowships with God and the Holy Spirit freely. Truly, he is the one housing the Godhead (God the Father, Son and the Holy Spirit).

a) But, the other half of our heart (the Soul- made up of mind, will and emotion) is not regenerated, as stated earlier. He is the fellow that is desperately wicked, carnal and sinful. This is why the Bible recommends and instructs that:

ii) The mind must constantly be renewed with the word of God and by the power of the Holy Spirit (Romans 12:2; Ephesians 4:23; Philippians 2:5, 12- 13).

a) And our will trained to be subject to, and line up with the will of God, always (Romans 12:3). All men (believers and unbelievers), have strong and rebellious will that must be submitted to the will of God.

b) Also our emotions must be harnessed and subjected to

the fruit of the spirit, for the purpose of stability (Galatians 5:22, 23).

Our unregenerated (unsaved) soul creates room for spiritual warfare (11 Corinthians 10:3-6). So, the greatest challenge facing a believer in serving God and in enforcing his authority over Satan; is a mind that need to be renewed, and a will that need to become obedient to the word of God, and emotion that need to be stabilized. The purpose of this exercise is to achieve alignment of the soul and our new creation spirit. Our body also has to be subjected to the word and be presented as a living sacrifice (1 Corinthians 9:27; Romans 12:1, 2).

"And the very God of peace sanctify you wholly; and I pray God your whole spirit and soul and body be preserved blameless unto the coming of our Lord Jesus." (1 Thessalonians 5:23).

Authoritative, powerful, victorious and spiritual life style of a believer demands a spiritual synergy of our spirit, soul and body. All three members of our being must consciously be trained to function in one accord. Otherwise, our house is divided and constantly at war - *"for the flesh lusteth against the Spirit and the Spirit against the flesh."* (Galatians 5:17). This is the climax of spiritual conflict and warfare in our life and can only be resolved when we get our glorious body. Satan takes advantage of this error.

As for the unbelievers, the totality of their heart (spirit, soul) is desperately wicked because they are not regenerated and are still in darkness. All unbelievers are adamic by nature and spiritually dead (Acts 26:14-18; Eph 2:1-6; 4:17-18). Therefore, the wickedness of the heart of a man, according to the Bible, refers completely (spirit and soul) to the unbelievers; and partially (soul only) to the believers in Christ.

Let's see another scripture, as we continue our analysis of the biblical meaning of the heart of a man. When the Bible says, *"Keep thy heart with all diligence; for out of it are the issues of life"*. (Proverbs 4:23 KJV), we know that God is referring to the invisible organ of man (spirit and soul), because both are responsible for the destiny and the course of the life of a man. The spirit of a man, enables him to function in the realm of the spirit and to communicate with spiritual beings. While his soul (personality), using his body; enables him to function in the physical planet earth and also interact with the inhabitants. Interestingly, the spiritual realm is not only more real than the natural realm, but it's also more powerful and controls the natural realm of existence.

The spiritual realm is not only more real than the natural realm, but it's also more powerful and controls the natural realm of existence.

No man can exercise dominion on earth except he has knowledge of the spiritual realm. We must not forget that man is a spirit being, who has a soul and dwells in a physical human body.

The Mind of a Believer and Faith:

With regards to faith, we focus mainly on the mind of a believer for two major reasons:

a) The spirit of a believer is righteous, holy, full of faith (gifts of faith, faith from the fruit of the spirit and also from the gift of the Spirit, if qualified by the Holy Spirit), and houses the living word (Jesus). This spirit is a perfect man of faith. We don't have issues of faith with Him (1 Peter 3:3-4; Ephesians 4:24; Colossians 3:10; Romans 8:23).

But the soul (mind, will and emotion) is not born again and remains selfish and fleshly (James 1:21; Hebrews 10:39). We however focus on the mind because the mind drives the will and emotions and indirectly controls the body and the affairs of man.

All three members of our being must consciously be trained to function in one accord. Otherwise, our house is divided and constantly at war.

So many scriptures reveal that faith fundamentally is the issue of the heart (mind). One of the many earlier referenced is Mark 11:23 where we are told that when a person speaks to the mountain and does "....*not doubt in his heart, but shall believe...*" it shall come to pass. We are also aware that believing is a matter of the heart.

"For with the heart man believeth unto righteousness; and with the mouth confession is made unto salvation." (Romans 10:10 KJV).

Also, 11 Corinthians 4:13 declares:

"We having the same spirit of faith, according as it is written, I

believed, and therefore have I spoken; we also believe, and therefore speak."

The heart (mind) therefore, is the arena where faith (the substance and evidence of our reality), belief (corresponding action of faith), and doubt (opposite of faith) perform their operation. Even the speaking (confession) aspect of faith, according to Christ is a product of the heart (mind). This is revealed when Christ said:

"*O generation of vipers, how can ye, being evil, speak good things? for out of the abundance of the heart the mouth speaketh.*" (Matthew 12:34 KJV).

Also in Matthew 6:31 (KJV), He (Christ) said:

"*Therefore take no thought, saying, What shall we eat? or, What shall we drink? Or, Wherewithal shall we be clothed?*"

Invariably, the heart (mind) constitutes a mighty pillar in the realm of faith. If our mind is corrupted, our faith will be corrupted. As a result the Bible encourages us to shun the spirit of fear and embrace a sound mind.

"*For God hath not given us the spirit of fear; but of power, and of love, and of a sound mind.*" (11 Timothy 1:7 KJV)

If our mind is unstable, our faith will be unstable. Hence, Apostle James warns us saying:

"*If any of you lack wisdom* (or anything), *let him ask of God, that giveth to all men liberally, and upbraideth not; and it shall be given him.*

But let him ask in faith, nothing wavering. For he that wavereth is like a wave of the sea driven with the wind and tossed.

For let not that man think (mindset) that he shall receive anything of the Lord.

A double minded man is unstable in all his ways." (James 1: 5-8 KJV)

Definitely, unstable or double mind will generate unstable faith, unstable expectations, unstable results, and an unstable life. But a sound, stable mind will support and produce a stable and effective faith that can move mountains. Jesus, before the cross, did not ignore the importance of stable and sound heart (mind) in our faith lifestyle. Hence, He lovingly cautioned:

"Let not your heart (mind) *be troubled: ye believe* (faith) *in God, believe also in me."* (John 14:1 KJV)

A troubled, unstable, and unsound heart (mind) definitely will kill your belief, which is the corresponding action of faith. Many have given up in their faith saying: "I don't have faith" or that their faith is ineffective simply because they are ignorant of the role of the mind in the operation of faith. In 1 Thessalonians 3:10 (KJV), Apostle Paul said,

"Night and day praying exceedingly that we might see your face, and might perfect that which is lacking in your faith?"

I believe, among the things the Apostle was referring to, as missing in our faith is a sound mind. In our life as the new creation, the most unstable organ is the mind. In dealing with the supernatural armor of a spiritual warrior of Christ, the Bible describes our mind as "Loins":

"Stand therefore, having your loins girt about with truth, and having on the breastplate of righteousness." (Ephesians 6:14 KJV). 1Peter1:13 explains that loins refer to our mind:

"Wherefore gird up the loins of your mind, be sober, and hope to the end for the grace that is to be brought unto you at the revelation of Jesus Christ."

Also, Apostle James confirms that when he said: "A double minded man is unstable in all his ways." (James 1:8) and shall not receive any thing of the Lord (James 1:7). Indeed, unstable mind is a faithless mind.

We thank God for the Holy Spirit's revelation of the scriptures and also scriptures that interpret scriptures. Our mind is described as a loin and we all know that the loin is most flexible and unstable. We are encouraged to police and stabilize our mind with the truth of the gospel (the word of faith).

If our mind is unstable, our faith will be unstable.

Let us make another observation in Philippians 4:6-7 (KJV). Here, we are told:

"Be careful for nothing; but in everything by prayer and supplication with thanksgiving let your requests be made known unto God.

And the peace of God, which passeth all understanding, shall keep your hearts and minds through Christ Jesus."

This scripture signifies that our hearts and minds are mostly and easily targeted and assaulted by our enemies (the forces of darkness-Satan, demons, the world, challenges, temptations etc.), even our flesh (senses). Hence, the battle of the mind. Of course another strategy to maintaining a sound mind is..."*Looking* (focusing) *unto Jesus the author and finisher of our faith.*" (Hebrews 12:2a KJV)

"*Set your affection* (mind) *on things above, not on things on earth. For ye are dead, and your life is hid with Christ in God.*" (Colossians 3:2, 3 KJV)

One will never experience a productive faith life without a sound mind that is not distracted from the author and finisher of our faith. Not setting our mind on Christ only, will constitute double mindedness, which makes faith unproductive.

In our life as the new creation, the most unstable organ is the mind. In dealing with the supernatural armor of a spiritual warrior of Christ, the Bible describes our mind as "Loins".

I will not close this section without exposing Satan's diabolic plot against the mind of the righteous and hence, our faith, once again for the sake of emphasis. Because our faith is our offensive (1 John 5:4) and defensive (Ephesians 6:16) weapon of victory against the devil, he plots to undermine our faith by unleashing relentless and insidious attack on our minds. He carries out this satanic campaign together with his evil regiment called seducing spirits. The following scriptures are very helpful:

"*But I fear, lest by any means, as the serpent beguiled Eve*

through his subtlety, so your minds should be corrupted from the simplicity that is in Christ." (11 Corinthians 11:3 KJV).

The corruption of our minds here refers to the manipulative and deceitful strategy and activity of Satan against our unregenerated minds; with the intention of reducing our mind to a fruitless barren platform of faith. Hence, the Bible emphasizes on the renewing of our minds and taking of thought into captivity to the obedience of Christ and the word of God.

How about the activities of demonic forces of Satan? The Bible calls them seducing spirits. Yes, they are busy, powerfully manipulating and enticing the minds of gullible, sometimes innocent and spiritually bankrupt people as seen below:

"Now the Spirit speaketh expressly, that in the latter times some shall depart from the faith, giving heed to seducing spirits, and doctrines of devils." (I Timothy 4:1 KJV)

Glory be to God for the abundance of revelation available to us in the Holy Scriptures. From this we come to know that the massive influx of wrong doctrines and deceitful signs and wonders in our local churches, the incredible lukewarmness, corruption and unprecedented number of backsliding Christians are the results of the seducing activities of demons on our minds. So they seduce our minds to rebel against our creator and our redeemer, our savior Jesus Christ, and the Holy Spirit of promise with whom God has sealed us; as well as the word of God.

What can we say, concerning their (seducing spirits) catastrophic assault and abuse of the minds of the ungodly? Wars and rumors of wars, terrorism, shootings, prostitution, drug abuse, and all the vices and atrocities plaguing humanity are the activities of Satan and seducing spirits in the minds of people. This abysmal tragedy of mankind started in the Garden of Eden, and was preceded by the similar calamity that befell one-third of the angels in heaven. Unfortunately, these seduced and fallen angels became the seducing spirits of the heavenlies troubling the inhabitants of the planet earth. The book of Revelation 12:12 gives us insight:

"Therefore rejoice, ye heavens, and ye that dwell in them. Woe to the inhabiters of the earth and of the sea! for the devil is come down unto you, having great wrath, because he knoweth that he hath but short time."

Our gratitude to God for His plan of redemption will never diminish.

By diligently guarding the loins of our minds with the word of faith we will maintain a sound mind and overthrow any plot to undermine our faith, by the defeated ancient treacherous foe - the devil and his cohorts (all labeled seducing spirits).

A sound, stable mind will support and produce a stable and effective faith that can move mountains.

Beloved, this is revelation knowledge of spiritual warfare. It's called, pulling down strongholds, casting down imaginations, and taking all thoughts captive (II Corinthians 10:3-5).

Sound mind begets sound faith!

Although the devil is disarmed (Colossians 2:14-15), don't forget that he has perfected his weapons of manipulative, deceitful craftiness and strategies. The Bible calls them lying vanities (Jonah 2:8) and we are vulnerable to these because his profitable battle field is our mind. We're warned about his craftiness and hidden agenda in 11 Corinthians 2:11 (KJV):

"Lest Satan should get advantage of us: for we're not ignorant of his devices."

Anytime you succumb to the lies of the devil coming through your mind or other diverse sources, definitely he will take advantage of you as the Bible says:

"And he shall speak great words against the most High, and shall wear out the saints of the most High,....." (Daniel 7:25a KJV). How?

Speaking great words against the Most High and wearing out the saints all take place in our minds. The devil understands what the Bible said about the mind of the new creation in Romans 7:25b KJV):

"I thank God through Jesus Christ our Lord.

So with the mind, I myself serve the Law of God; but with the flesh the law of sin."

"*But I see another law in my members, warring agaist the law of my mind, and bringing me into captivity to the law of sin which is in my members.*" (Romans 7:23).

Recalling the previous scriptures that reveal that Satan corrupts our minds, while his demons seduce our minds; we discover that these forces of darkness are responsible for the destructive thoughts that draw humanity away from God and provoke wars and atrocities among the inhabitants of the earth.

153

Why do powers of darkness target our minds? They target our minds because, corruption and failure of the mind is responsible for faithlessness in our lives. I conclude this section with this relevant biblical prayer request:

"Finally, brethren, pray for us, that the word of the Lord may have free course, and be glorified, even as it is with you. And that we may be delivered from unreasonable and wicked men: for all men have not faith." (11 Thessalonians 3:1, 2).

Without controversy, the unreasonableness and wickedness of man is a result of lack of faith; which in turn, is a product of the battle of the mind. This battle, no doubt, is originated, and masterminded by the forces of evil.

The massive influx of wrong doctrines and deceitful signs and wonders in our local churches, the incredible lukewarmness, corruption and unprecedented number of backsliding Christians are the results of the seducing activities of demons on our minds.

Unfortunately, many are yet to be alerted, enlightened and to understand that, ungodly, sinful, offensive and negative thoughts and thinking patterns are not our thoughts. They originate from our enemies. They are the products of relentless assault of deception and manipulation by Satan and his demons in our minds. What do we do with them? Just follow divine instruction of casting them down and bringing them into captivity to the obedience of Christ (11 Corinthians 10:3-6).

If you are lazy and permit them to graduate to strongholds; you must pull them down without delay. Also learn how to instantly replace thoughts with what the Bible says about you. Out- rightly refuse to consider or meditate on negative, ungodly and sinful thoughts. If you mistakenly consider them, repent immediately and consider the relevant promises of God that contradict them.

A productive faith life requires a mind that is renewed with the word of faith, because:

1) Faith is believing, confessing and acting on the word of faith, which is the word of God.

2) Also, faith comes by hearing the word of faith.

CHAPTER 20
STEADFASTNESS - PILLAR OF OUR FAITH

Steadfastness, no doubt is a missing pillar in the faith tabernacle of many. How can a Christ-like spiritual warrior who is permanently deployed in the warfare and battle field of faith ignore the warning in the following scriptures?

1)*"Submit yourselves therefore to God. Resist the devil, and he will flee from you."* (James 4:7)

"Be sober, be vigilant; because your adversary the devil, as a roaring lion, walketh about, seeking whom he may devour.

Whom (the devil) *resist stedfast in the faith, knowing that the same afflictions are accomplished in your brethren that are in the world."* (I Peter 5:8-9 KJV)

We're in a warfare where the ceasefire is a delusion and all our opposing combatants are naturally and spiritually relentless. In short, they are oppressively consistent, and they can be factored into a constant. Following the above, the Bible employs very powerful and strong militant verbs and adjectives to qualify our strategies. They are: *"submit,"* *"resist,"* *"sober,"* *"vigilant,"* and *"steadfast."*

Accordingly, we must resist the enemy. But how do we resist the enemy? The answer and command is: by being steadfast. Again with

what?- the weapon and armor of faith. This is the point where faith-failure rests in many. The instruction is that the enemy must be resisted steadfastly by faith. To resist means to withstand. Imagine a situation where one relaxes or temporarily withdraws his "withstanding." No doubt the incident of casualty will be reported.

We must recall that faith is the over-comer's offensive weapon of victory and a defensive shield of armor to a kingdom warrior, as recorded below:

"For what so sever is born of God over cometh the world: and this is the victory that over cometh the world, even our faith." (I John 5:4 KJV)

"Above all, taking the shield of faith, wherewith ye shall be able to quench all the fiery darts of the wicked." (Ephesians 6:16 KJV).

What will happen to the offensive attack and the fiery darts of the wicked when our offensive victory weapon of faith is temporarily quieted, or when our defensive and protective shield of faith is momentarily laid down to rest? In the above circumstance how many fiery darts of the enemy will locate the Calvary Warriors and what will be the magnitude of the casualty in our camp? To some people, the previous comments may seem to be partakers of exaggeration but as a truth, they are realities of our daily experience.

A whole lot of believers are releasing their faith against their enemies in unfavorable circumstances and situations, but not with a steadfast progressive strategy. Our adversaries must be resisted steadfastly by faith (I Peter 5:9). In other words, the agenda of the operation of our faith must be the agenda of stability and consistency. Let me conclude this section with Apostle Paul's admonishment on this issue in Colossians 2:4 - 8 (KJV):

"And this I say, lest any man should beguile you with enticing words.

For though I be absent in the flesh, yet am I with you in the spirit, joying and beholding your order, and the stedfastness of your faith in Christ.

As ye have therefore received Christ Jesus the Lord, so walk ye in him.

Rooted and built up in him, and established in the faith, as ye have been taught, abounding therein with thanksgiving.

Beware lest any man spoil you through philosophy and vain deceit, after the tradition of men, after the rudiments of the world, and not after Christ."

Notice the following from the writing of Paul:

1. We must shun teachings and doctrines that contradict the word of faith of the gospel of Christ. In other words, we must not allow enticing words of man's wisdom to undermine the benefits of the cross. Without the cross, our faith is limited to human natural faith, which is subject to failure.
2. Our faith must be steadfast and the point of focus must be Christ - the author and finisher of our faith.

3. The eternal life we received from God through Christ must be lived according to the way we received Christ. How did we receive Christ - by grace through faith and in the spirit, since we did not see Christ in the natural? (Ephesians 2:8, 9)? We must be rooted and built up in Christ. This refers to our spiritual growth of transformation till Christ is formed in us (Romans 12:1, 2; Ephesians 4:11-15; Galatians 4:1-3, 19). We must be established in faith, and grow it to a level of stability.
4. Successful and victorious life of faith is sustained by thanksgiving and glorious praises like Abraham - our father of faith (Romans 4:16-25).

Elijah and Elisha:

What can we say about Elisha as it pertains to the steadfastness of faith? Step-by-step analysis of a biblical incident will suffice. God purposed to take Elijah to heaven in a whirlwind, and then Elijah went with Elisha from Gilgal (II Kings 2:1). As he was about to leave, Elijah instructed Elisha to remain in Gilgal because God has sent him to Bethel. Elisha responded with a strong statement thus: "...*As the Lord liveth, and as thy soul liveth, I will not leave thee.....*" (11 Kings 2:2 KJV). When they arrived at Bethel, another barrage of the trail against his faith came through the sons of prophets. And he replied: "*Yea, I know it; hold ye your peace.*" (11 Kings 2:3 KJV)

The trend continued, but thank God by His persistent faith, he made it to Jericho, and handled the question of the sons of the prophets there in the same manner "*Yea, I know it; hold ye your peace.*" (11 Kings 2:5 KJV). Elijah himself again instructed him to remain in Jericho while he proceeded to Jordan. But Elisha refused to give up his faith of becoming a prophet of double standard to

Elijah (11 Kings 2:6). Behold another set of sons of prophets emerged, this time numbering up to fifty spectators - hanging on the wings to potentially become possible hindrance to the steadfastness of Elisha's faith. He survived this onslaught too.

However, when Elijah miraculously divided the Jordan river with his mantle, Elisha faithfully and fearlessly crossed over with him on dry ground; not minding how he would make it back (II Kings 2:8). Even the body and waves of the Jordan River could not undermine Elisha's tenacious resolve and steadfastness of faith. In this process indeed, Elisha demonstrated to us that steadfast faith is a champion.

After they had successfully crossed over the Jordan River, Elijah requested Elisha to petition his need. Elisha then demanded double portion of his anointing. Prior to the victory over Jordan, Elijah offered nothing to Elisha and Elisha himself had no opportunity to make any request. Hence, he had no tangible promise driving him to follow.

But glory be to God, the encounter ended with Elisha being clothed with the double portion of Elijah's anointing. This encounter is a fascinating and supernatural account of the potency and capabilities of faith released under the pillar and nourishment of steadfastness.

Elisha and the Shunamite Woman:

The case of Elisha, the Shunamite woman, and the death and resurrection of her son is another fascinating account of the role and power of steadfastness in the operation of victorious and adamant faith.

As recorded in the Bible, the son of this generous Shunamite woman, who was a product of the miraculous, died when Elisha was not scheduled to be in their community. But this spiritual woman of faith (unlike her husband) steadfastly set her adamant faith in motion - searching for the prophet. Eventually the man of God was located by faith and he delegated Gehazi (his servant) to the mission of the resurrection of the young lad. But unfortunately, the mission ended in a failure (11 Kings 4:29-31). One would think that he (Elisha) would have permitted a funeral then, but the prophet was relentless. His relentlessness and steadfastness was authored as follows:

"And when Elisha was come into the house, behold the child was dead, and laid upon his bed. He went in therefore, and shut the door upon them twain, and prayed unto the Lord.

And he went up, and lay upon the child, and put his mouth upon his mouth, and his eyes upon his eyes, and his hands upon his hands: and he stretched himself upon the child; and the flesh of the child waxed warm." (11 Kings 4:32-34 KJV).

Despite his diligent and stubborn application of faith, there was no resurrection. But the Prophet was relentless and steadfast. The Bible records that: *"he returned, and walked in the house to and fro; and went up, and stretched himself upon him: and the boy sneezed seven times, and the child opened his eyes."* (11 Kings 4:35 KJV). Alas! Resurrection responded to persistent faith and steadfastness. The mission was accomplished to God's glory.

In another scenario, a density of antagonistic crowd attempting to silence blind Bartimaeus was shamelessly paralyzed by relentless steadfast faith. These fellows were wicked and unreasonable people who had no faith - (11 Thessalonians 3:2).

According to eye witness account: "when *he heard that it was Jesus of Nazareth, he began to cry out, and say, Jesus, thou son of David, have mercy upon me. And many charged him that he should hold his peace: but he cried the more a great deal, Thou son of David, have mercy on me.*

And Jesus said unto him, Go thy way; thy faith hath made thee whole. And immediately he received his sight, and followed Jesus in the way." (Mark 10:47-48, 52 KJV)

A successful and victorious life of faith is sustained by thanksgiving and glorious praises like Abraham - our father of faith (Romans 4:16-25).

Steadfast faith which I call the steadfastness of faith paid off in the life of Bartimaeus, and it can in yours too if you apply it in your desperate situation. Steadfast faith has a dynamic creative power for signs and wonders, and in all the cases testified previously, it demonstrated and proved to be an agent of the miraculous. The Holy Spirit is our helper, and I pray: Holy Spirit, please help us not to toy with steadfastness in our faith, endeavors and encounters. In conclusion, please note that steadfastness is a pillar of faith, period.

CHAPTER 21
BOLDNESS - PILLAR OF FAITH

"**T**he wicked flee when no man pursueth: but the *righteous are bold as a lion.*" (Proverbs 28:1 KJV)

Since the righteous is programmed to live by faith (Habakkuk 2:4; Romans 1:17, Galatians 3:11; Hebrews 10:38), the boldness of the righteous is the boldness of faith. Faith and boldness are also inseparable. How do you account for David's audacity of faith towards Goliath of Gath? When the Hebrew slave boys were indicted in Babylon by King Nebuchadnezzar, and sentenced to agonizing death in a burning fiery furnace; below is their documented phraseology of boldness of faith.

"Shadrach, Meshach, and Abednego, answered and said to the king. O Nebuchadnezzar, we are not careful to answer thee in this matter.

If it be so our God whom we serve is able to deliver us from the burning fiery furnace, and he will deliver us out of thine hand, O King.

But if not, be it known unto thee, O king, that we will not serve thy gods, nor worship the golden image which thou hast set up." (Daniel 3:16-18)

These young men indeed launched targeted supernatural and ballistic missiles of faith, saturated and decorated with the inexplicable roses of boldness. That was not ordinary, but divine boldness. Boldness is not only a pillar of faith, but like righteousness, it is also a gift of God. Faith is the most potent force in the universe. But without boldness faith ceases to be a force.

Believers' Dominion Over Principalities and Powers in Heavenly Places:

Many scriptures teach that God through Christ Jesus has given us (the new creation) authority, power, and dominion over principalities and powers. A Few of the scriptures are:

"And when he had called unto him his twelve disciples, he gave them power against unclean spirits, to cast them out, and to heal all manner of sickness and all manner of disease." (Matthew 10:1 KJV)

"And these signs shall follow them that believe; In my name shall they cast out devils; they shall speak with new tongues;

They shall take up serpents; and if they drink any deadly thing, it shall not hurt them; They shall lay hands on the sick, and they shall recover." (Mark 16:17-18 KJV).

"And the seventy returned again with joy, saying, Lord, even the devils are subject unto us through thy name.

And he said unto them, I beheld Satan as lightning fall from heaven.

Behold, I give unto you power (authority) to tread on serpents and scorpions, and over all the power of the enemy: and nothing shall by any means hurt you." (Luke 10:17-19 KJV)

It's amazing and exciting to see and know the amount of authority, power, and dominion we have received from God over the powers of darkness. But the Bible also makes it very clear that these powers and dominion can only be exercised through faith in our Lord Jesus Christ. Without doubt we do have available to us the faith of Christ (Galatians 2:16, 20).

Steadfast faith has a dynamic creative power for signs and wonders.

Unfortunately, one of the things that is missing in the proficiency of our faith is boldness. Apostle Paul mentioned this, when he requested for prayer, saying: pray for me, *"that utterance may be given unto me that I may open my mouth boldly, to make known the mystery of the gospel. For which I am an ambassador in bonds: that therein I may speak boldly, as I ought to speak."* (Ephesians 6:19, 20).

Scriptures also conspicuously state that our ability to rule over principalities and powers is dependent on our boldness and confidence in the faith of Christ. The scripture speaks for itself as we read below:

"To the intent that now unto the principalities and powers in

heavenly places might be known by the church the manifold wisdom of God,

According to the eternal purpose which he purposed in Christ Jesus our Lord:

In whom we have boldness and access with confidence by the faith of him (Christ)." (Ephesians 3:10-12 KJV).

We see from the scripture above that boldness gives us access to and confidence in the faith of Christ, which in turn gives us the authority and power over principalities and powers.

How do you account for David's audacity of faith towards Goliath of Gath?

I suppose, without boldness in her faith, precipitated by three days of prayer and fasting, Queen Esther could not have been able to; without penalty of death: break King Ahasuerus visitation laws and orders. Boldness in her faith no doubt provoked the divine intervention that aborted Haman's satanic plot against the Jews. This story, as recorded in the book of Esther, is another fascinating account of the dynamic power of boldness as a pillar of faith: that is, boldness in action.

Space does not permit me to chronicle Daniel's showcase of boldness in the execution of his faith while in Babylonian captivity. Daniel did become the prophetic mouthpiece of God in a heathen world and culture. The Bible records:

"Now when Daniel knew that the writing was signed, he went into his house; and his windows being open in his chamber toward Jerusalem, he kneeled upon his knees three times a day, and prayed, and gave thanks before his God as he did aforetime." (Daniel 6:10 KJV).

A fearful man cannot attempt what Daniel did. Without exaggeration, Daniel's action was a supernatural display of audacity of boldness in faith. The Holy Spirit, through Apostle Paul, also educated us on the important relationship between our faith and boldness. And this is recorded in I Timothy 3:13 (HCSB):

"For those who have served well as deacons acquire a good standing for themselves, and great boldness in the faith that is in Christ Jesus."

Indeed great boldness is required as a catalytic pillar in successful and productive execution of our faith. No wonder, Jesus, recognizing the boldness of the widow before the unjust Judge; also lamented in Luke 18:8: saying: *"Nevertheless when the Son of man cometh, shall he find faith on the earth?"*

Recalling the healing episode of the paralytic, the Bible recorded:

"Since they could not get him to Jesus because of the crowd, they made an opening in the roof above Jesus by digging through it and then lowered the mat the man was lying on." (Mark 2:4 NIV)

Thinking about this provocative action, then I ask: how could one have done this fearlessly without boldness? However,

"When Jesus saw their faith, he said unto the sick of the palsy, Son thy sins be forgiven thee.

I say unto thee, Arise, and take up thy bed, and go thy way into thine house.

And immediately he arose, took up the bed, and went forth before them all; insomuch that they were all amazed, and glorified God, saying, We never saw it on this fashion." (Mark 2:5, 11-12 KJV)

These young men indeed launched targeted supernatural and ballistic missiles of faith, saturated and decorated with the inexplicable roses of boldness.

This is what boldness can contribute to our act of faith. May we not lock up our boldness in our closets as we go about, attempting to move mountains by faith in Jesus name. Amen.

CHAPTER 22
PERSUASION - PILLAR OF FAITH

P ersuasion is a pillar of faith. It's also a deep-rooted conviction - a firmly held view.

Persuasion can also be defined as advanced belief. That's a belief with no room for doubt and unbelief. Abraham's faith was operatively unstable until persuasion was incorporated in his faith portfolio as earlier described, examined, reviewed and severally analyzed in some parts of this book. These are all recorded in Romans 4:20-24.

"He staggered not at the promise of God through unbelief; but was strong in faith, giving glory to God; And being fully persuaded that, what he had promised, he was able also to perform. And therefore it was imputed to him for righteousness. Now it was not written for his sake alone, that it was imputed to him; But for us also, to whom it shall be imputed, if we believe on him that raised up Jesus our Lord from the dead."

It's not difficult to realize that without persuasion, Abraham corrupted his faith when he detoured to procreate the promised child through Hagar. And instead of Isaac, Ishmael showed up. But according to Romans 4:20-21 when Abraham became fully persuaded that God is faithful concerning his promises, the promised spiritual child (Isaac) was born.

"*He* (Abraham) *staggered not at the promise of God through unbelief; but was strong in faith, giving glory to God. And being fully persuaded that, what He had promised, He was able to perform.*"

When Abraham became fully persuaded that God is faithful concerning his promises, the promised spiritual child (Isaac) was born.

Furthermore, with the power of persuasion, Abraham was able to overcome unbelief and weakness of faith. Concerning Abraham and faith, we must learn that any attempt to release faith without the power of persuasion will create room for doubt, unbelief, and weakness of faith. The Bible strongly declares that Abraham became not just persuaded, but fully persuaded that God is able to perform. Ephesians 3:20 (KJV) states that God:

"*Is able to do exceeding abundantly above all that we ask or think, according to the power that worketh in us.*"

What power is referred to above? No doubt, it is the power of persuasion of the Holy Spirit which is working mightily in all believers in Christ (Colossians 1:27-29). This power also includes the power of the word of God as disclosed by 1 Thessalonians 2:13 (NIV) saying,

"And we also thank God continually because, when you received the word of God, which you heard from us, you accepted it not as a human word, but as it actually is, the word of God, which is indeed at work in you who believe."

This is the same power that raised Christ from the dead. Ephesians 1:19 and 20 described this power as exceedingly great and mighty power. The word of God also persuasively encourages us to exercise adamant faith in God. This becomes very clear when Paul defended himself before the Roman consulate in Acts 26:24-26.

"And as he (Paul) thus spake for himself, Festus said with a loud voice, Paul, thou art beside thyself; much learning doth make thee mad.

But he said, I am not mad, most noble, Festus; but speak forth the words of truth and soberness.

For the king knoweth of these things, before whom also I speak freely: for I am persuaded that none of these things are hidden from him; for this thing was not done in a corner."

Then he concluded saying:

"King Agrippa, believest thou the prophets? I know that thou believest.

Then Agrippa said unto Paul, Almost thou persuadest me to be a Christian." (Acts 26:27-28 KJV)

Please notice that the persuasive force of faith that is capable of moving mountains, operative in Apostle Paul; greatly influenced King Agrippa. But the spiritual stronghold of blindness and darkness [which are the products of Satan himself (Acts 26:18)]; robbed King Agrippa the gift of eternal life.

Any attempt to release faith without the power of persuasion will create rooms for doubt, unbelief, and weakness of faith.

As recorded in 11 Corinthians 4:4, Satan is responsible for the stubborn will and stony heart that prevail against the gospel of Christ in all unbelievers. This disastrous agenda of Satan, qualify every unbeliever as a natural man who does not understand or receive the things of the Holy Spirit (1 Corinthians 2:14).

Alas! Agrippa was robbed of the most valuable gift ever presented to humanity on the planet earth - the gift of eternal life from God through Christ Jesus.

Indeed, strong and productive faith requires the strength of persuasion. Queen Esther, as recorded in the Bible, once said:

"Go, gather together all the Jews that are present in Shushan, and fast ye for me, and neither eat nor drink three days, night or day: I also and my maidens will fast likewise; and so will I go in unto the king, which is not according to the law: and if I perish, I perish." (Esther 4:16 KJV)

What! *"If I perish, I perish."* Esther indeed operated her faith under the platform of the power of persuasion. Mordecai's (Esther's uncle) encouragement activated this power in Esther and her corresponding action of faith provoked amazing divine intervention that brought historic deliverance to the Jews.

Do you know that many who commit suicide would have been living if they were tutored through the power of persuasion? No matter what we go through - no matter how hurting, discouraged, or depressed we may be, we should learn to be fully persuaded, like Abraham, that help is always on the way. Our God is a faithful and miraculous God. He is also a Father, and He will never leave us, nor forsake us (Hebrews 13:5). His persuasive word of faith stands forever (Isaiah 40:8). And He (God) is never late. He specializes in divine intervention, and He once said,

"Behold, I am the Lord, the God of all flesh: is there anything too hard for me?" (Jeremiah 32:27 KJV).

Indeed, there is nothing He cannot subdue on our behalf. As a matter of the truth, the Bible says:

"For the eyes of the Lord run to and fro throughout the whole earth, to shew himself strong in the behalf of them whose heart is perfect toward him." (11 Chronicles 16:9a KJV)

There's no doubt God is more concerned and more willing than we are; concerning our deliverance and the overthrow of our enemies. We will become more than persuaded if we consider the power of persuasion displayed by the Hebrew boys in Babylonian captivity - as they released their adamant faith.

Strong and productive faith requires the strength of persuasion.

Then and there, they decreed and declared to King Nebuchadnezar their unshakable decision based on the power of persuasion (Daniel 3:16-17 KJV). In a nutshell they convincingly declared *"And he will deliver us out of thine hand."* Wow! What a density of persuasion. I guess, they were saying,

"We're overwhelmingly and tenaciously persuaded that our God will deliver us." And if not, we will not consider your command. Can you see the way they responded to the most powerful personality of that era? This is persuasive faith in action.

That notwithstanding, the king commanded the furnace to be heated seven times above normal. Unfortunately for the king, because their faith was powerfully supported by the pillar of persuasion, there was no room for fear or unbelief. Recall that they even served a notice to the king, saying:

"But if not, be it known unto thee, O king, that we will not serve thy gods, nor worship the golden image which thou hast set up." (Daniel 3:18 KJV)

What was the outcome of this historic, notorious and treacherous trail of that generation? Of course the king, the whole kingdom celebrated their victory with them. Are you ready and persuaded to consistently celebrate your victory and freedom in every department of your life and in any circumstance; in the midst of your enemies and in the precious name of Jesus? But very interesting and amazing was the king's remarks. The Bible succinctly declares in Daniel 3:24-25 that:

"Then Nebuchadnezzar the king was astonished, and rose up in haste, and spake, and said unto his counsellors, Did not we cast three men bound into the midst of the fire? They answered and said unto the king,

True, O king. He answered and said, Lo, I see four men loose, walking in the midst of the fire, and they have no hurt; and the form of the fourth is like the Son of God." (Daniel 3: 24-25 KJV)

Behold, three men bound were cast into the fire. But the redeemer invaded the furnace and the four freely walked in the midst of adversity and the King had uncommon opportunity to see the Son of God. He was dazed with glorious supernatural eyesight that gave him insight into the realm of the spiritual. When you enforce persuasion as a faith dynamic, even your adversaries will partake of the resultant miraculous feat.

No matter what we go through - no matter how hurting, discouraged, or depressed we may be, we should learn to be fully persuaded, like Abraham, that help is always on the way.

What a joyful revelation for the redeemed: that even before redemption the promise of supernatural protection was recorded in many places in the Bible and is effective as the covenant "of the day and the night". Jesus, in Matthew 28:20 declared: *"Lo, I am with you alway, even unto the end of the world."*

"I will never leave thee, nor forsake thee." (Hebrews 13:5 KJV)

The divine record is: It's finished (John19:30). All power is given unto me in heaven and on earth. And behold, I give unto you authority over all the powers of the enemy. For the new creation, the redeemed of the most high, the Son of God is not only with us but He is in us for eternity; for nothing shall separate us from His everlasting love (Colossians 1:27; Galatians 3:27; John 15:5;

Jeremiah 31: 3). We have supernatural assurance of companionship. Before and after redemption, the son of God is always with us.

Following the above, we can consistently and confidently, like Apostle Paul, say,

"For I know whom I have believed, and am persuaded that he is able to keep that which I have committed unto him against that day." (11 Timothy 1:12c KJV).

Yes, great faith demands great persuasiveness. Now, are you ready to be persuaded and nothing but to be persuaded that:

"Faithful is He who has called you; it is He who shall perform it." (1 Thessalonians 5:24) and that

"Being confident of this very thing, that He who began a good work in you will complete it until the day of Christ Jesus." (Philippians 1:6)?

Job also said in Job 19:25-26 (KJV),

"For I know that my redeemer liveth, and that he shall stand at the latter day upon the earth:

And though after my skin worms destroy this body, yet in my flesh shall I see God."

Again and firmly, for effective and productive lifestyle of faith, we must become persuaded that our God *"...is able to do exceedingly abundantly above all that we ask or think, according to the power that worketh in us."* (Ephesians 3:20).

Also we are told in Numbers 23:19 that:

"He (God) is not a man that He should lie, neither the son of

man that He should repent. Has He said it, and would He not do it? Or, has He spoken and failed to make it good."

As sons and daughters of the most high God (11 Corinthians 6:18), in the course of releasing our faith, we must always remember that all the promises of God in Christ Jesus are yes and amen (11 Corinthians 1:20). In other words, they are irrevocable. He unequivocally promised that He will not break His covenant concerning us; neither will He alter His promises over us. Rather He promised that He is vigilantly watching over His words to ensure their manifestation (Romans 11:29; Psalm 89:34; Jeremiah 1:12).

We're overwhelmingly and tenaciously persuaded that our God will deliver us.

In the battle of life, every believer must maintain the mindset that our faith, which is the weapon of our victory (1 John 5:4); must be persuasively and persistently engaged - realizing that Jesus is the originator and finisher of this faith. Moreover, Jesus is not only the creator of all things, but all things are for Him, exposed to Him, subject to Him and maintained by Him (Colossians 1:16; Hebrews 4:13; Hebrews 1:3).

CHAPTER 23
IMAGINATION - PILLAR OF FAITH

Imagination is a faculty of advanced thinking. It produces a mental picture of a concept, an idea, or an object that is not yet visible to the senses. Imagination is a pillar of faith and cannot be separated from faith since faith is the substance of things hoped for and evidence of things not seen. The domain of imagination is the mind. The mind has a dynamic creative power but imagination has a latent creative power. In other words, it has the ability and capacity to produce what is presently invisible to the senses.

A construction project of faith (our expectation), persistently supported by the pillar of imagination will definitely become a reality. God himself confirmed this in Genesis 11:1, 4-6 (KJV), saying:

"And the whole earth was of one language, and of one speech.

And they said, Go to, let us build us a city and a tower, whose top may reach unto heaven; and let us make us a name, lest we be scattered abroad upon the face of the whole earth.

And the Lord came down to see the city and the tower, which the children of men builded.

And the Lord said, Behold, the people is one, and they have all one language; and this they begin to do: <u>and now nothing will be restrained from them, which they have imagined to do.</u>"

"And now, nothing will be restrained from them which they have imagined to do."

This is a powerful revelation from a powerful God. Here, it's not difficult to learn from God that the latent (concealed) power of imagination breaks the power of hindrance and conquers the realm of impossibility. Again, *"..and nothing will be restrained from them, which they have imagined to do."*

Imagination is a faculty of advanced thinking. It produces a mental picture of a concept or an idea.

The mind as a thinking faculty and the domain of imagination has three faculties, or departments or dimension. They are:

1. Memory,
2. Meditation, and
3. Imagination.

All three are thinking or reasoning processes of which imagination is the most powerful. 11 Corinthians 10:3-5 describes negative or satanic imaginations as the building materials or resources for the construction of negative spiritual strongholds in our minds by satanic forces of evil.

"For though we walk in the flesh, we do not war after the flesh:

(For the weapons of our warfare are not carnal, but mighty through God to the pulling down of strongholds;)

Casting down imaginations, and every high thing that exalteth itself against the knowledge of God, and bringing into captivity every thought to the obedience of Christ." (11 Corinthians 10:3-5 KJV)

Negative spiritual strongholds are satanic or demonic pattern of thinking that have become a fortress (a fortified dwelling place) for the habitation of demons and demonic activities. These strongholds can also be described as mindsets impregnated with hopelessness, which causes the victims to believe and accept a lie that the seemingly hopeless situations are irreversible or unchangeable. This is what spiritual warfare is all about.

A simple ungodly (or sinful or negative) thought, uncontrolled or not arrested, with and by the relevant scriptures; grows and matures, and becomes a negative imagination. A negative imagination that is not cast down develops into a negative stronghold. And negative strongholds attract demonic strongman who brings in spirits of infirmities, suicide, poverty, divorce, fear, and very many others to relentlessly torment their victim. This (stronghold) becomes their safe and heavily guarded and protected residency. This satanic military strategy is called the battle of the mind.

But a positive and godly imagination fortifies and builds strong faith that provokes the manifestation of our expectations. As Abraham looked at the stars, believed God, and imagined himself as father of many nations; his faith produced a universal reality. Today, all the believers in Christ (world-wide) are the off-springs of Father Abraham. When next you exercise your faith, if a miracle eludes you, remember that you can invoke the power of the pillar of imagination to build your faith strong and sustain it until the manifestation of your reality.

The position of imagination in our human lifestyle of faith is too powerful. It determined, among the children of Israel in the wilderness, those who possessed the Promised Land, and those who didn't but perished in the wilderness. The Bible says in Hebrews 4:2 (KJV),

"For unto us was the gospel preached, as well as unto them: but the word preached did not profit them, not being mixed with faith in them that heard it."

As a result, they perished in the wilderness. What did they do? The ten spies that represented them saw (imagined) themselves as grasshoppers as recorded in Numbers 13:33 (KJV):

"And there we saw the giants, the sons of Anak, which come of the giants: and we were in our own sight (sight of the mind-imagination) as grasshoppers, and so we were in their sight."

This is terrible and unbelievable. The ten spies even went as far as concluding that the giants have taken them for grasshoppers. To me, this is a double-edged tragedy. These Jews were human beings but made themselves grasshoppers by negative imagination. Of course, the outcome of this ungodly negative imagination was a catastrophe. How powerful can imagination be?

In the bosom of their imagination (powerful determinant of faith), they drew and conclusively painted themselves as grasshoppers. Satanic and doubtful image of grasshoppers dethroned their faith. And the Almighty God of Jacob, the Holy One of Israel, permitted them to hop around the wilderness like grasshoppers until they all perished - not entering the Promised Land.

On the other hand, Joshua and Caleb saw the giants, but imagined that their supernatural miraculous God had taken away their strength, and transformed them into their daily bread.

"And Joshua the son of Nun, and Caleb the son of Jephunneh, which were of them that searched the land, ripped their clothes:

And they spake unto all the company of the children of Israel, saying, The land, which we passed through to search it, is an exceeding good land.

Only rebel not ye against the Lord, neither fear ye the people of the land; for they are bread for us: their defence is departed from them, and the Lord is with us: fear them not." (Numbers 14:6-7, 9 KJV).

Here, I learnt that negative imagination which produces faithlessness is a rebellion against God. The incident above is a practical illustration of the amalgamation of our imagination and our expectation. It's important to note that imagination is a powerful irrevocable faith in action. What is more, it (negative imagination) has the capacity to nullify our prayers, beliefs, and confessions. In other words, negative imaginations rank among the greatest hindrances to productive faith and prayer.

The recommendation is to ensure that negative and ungodly thoughts must be deleted (captured or arrested with the relevant word of God—11 Corinthians 10:3-5), before they develop into imagination, and later strongholds, according to scriptures.

Do not forget also that as a man thinks in his heart so is he (Proverbs 23:7). This is a spiritual law of God that is supportive of imagination. Imagination is advanced thinking process. It's a contemplative system that paints a mental picture of the expectation in the mind. It is also a seed that produces a reality. Once it is planted, the result is inevitable. Please, don't expect crop failure because this is a supernatural seed. The ball is in your court now.

Negative imagination which produces faithlessness is a rebellion against God.

Do not permit negative and ungodly imagination in your mind. They are not ordinary, but spiritual forces that war against the knowledge of the word of God in our lives according to scriptures (11 Corinthians 10:5). They also weaken and abort our faith and prayers.

"Keep your heart (mind) with all diligence; for out of it are the issues of life."(Proverbs4:23).

Issues of life originate from the heart (mind).

"A good man out of the good treasure of the heart (mind)

bringeth forth good things: and an evil man out of the evil treasure bringeth forth evil things (Matthew 12:35).

Good or evil things originate from the heart (mind).

"For from within, out of the heart (mind) of men, proceed evil thoughts, adulteries, fornications, murders, thefts, covetousness, wickedness, deceit, lasciviousness, an evil eye, blasphemy, pride, foolishness. All these evil things come from within, and defile the man." (Mark 7:21-23).

Evil things that defile a man are the products of thoughts which proceed from the heart (mind).

"For out of the abundance of the heart (mind) the mouth speaketh." (Matthew 12:34).

The heart (mind), speaks.

"Therefore take no thought, saying," (Matthew6:31).

The heart (mind) can say.

"Blessed are the pure in heart: for they shall see God."(Matthew 5:8).

The heart (mind) can see.

"But if our gospel be hid, it is hid to them that are lost; In whom the god of this world hath blinded the minds of them which believe not, less the light of the glorious gospel of Christ, who is the image of God, should shine unto them." (11 Corinthians 4:3, 4).

If the mind can be blinded, it can see.

"For as he thinketh in his heart, so is he." (Proverbs 23:7).

So the mind can think, see, speak, say, defile, be blinded, produce evil, good, and treasures; so can imagination. What a powerful component of man!

Imagination is advanced thinking process. It's a contemplative system that paints a mental picture of the expectation in the mind. It is also a seed that produces a reality. Once it is planted, the result is inevitable.

CHAPTER 24
THANKSGIVING - A PILLAR
OF FAITH

One of Apostle Paul's prayers narrates as thus:

"Night and day we pray most earnestly that we may see you again and supply what is lacking in your faith." (I Thessalonians 3:10 NIV).

I believe that thanksgiving is among the factors that are conspicuously absent in many believers' work of faith. Thanksgiving is indeed a pillar of faith. Faith constructed on the foundation of thanksgiving, executed or released by the logistics of thanksgiving, and watered, nourished and maintained by a relentless spring of thanksgiving, must irrevocably deliver our expectation.

As a result, Paul did not hesitate to caution the Colossians accordingly:

"So then, just as you received Christ Jesus as Lord, continue to live your lives in him, rooted and built up in him, strengthened

in the faith as you were taught, and overflowing with thankfulness." (Colossians 2:6-7 NIV)

This is a powerful revelation. If you want your faith to be strengthened, you must persistently overflow in thankfulness. So faith must be backed up by *"overflowing thankfulness."* No wonder many people's faith are aborted because they are supported by fear, stress, and anxiety, instead of thanksgiving.

Thanksgiving is among the factors that are conspicuously absent in many believers' work of faith. Thanksgiving is indeed a pillar of faith.

How true, clear, and adequate can the word of God be? Of a truth, you will know the truth, and the truth will set you free (John 8:32). However, it's the truth we know and practice that guarantees deliverance and freedom. Application of the truth in our daily life is what the Bible calls wisdom. Of course, *"Wisdom is the principal thing; therefore get wisdom: and with all thy getting get understanding."* (Proverbs 4:7 KJV)

From Abraham, we can learn a lot about the relationship between faith, thanksgiving and giving glory to God: as recorded in Romans 4:20: "*He* (Abraham) **staggered not at the promises of God through unbelief; but was strong in faith, giving glory to God."** "*Giving glory to God*" is the same as thanksgiving.

In Abraham's battle of faith, he *"gave glory to God."* Well, concerning the manifestation of Isaac, we all know that Abraham was confronted by monumental stronghold of time lag and delay. This was the primary factor that corrupted his faith and led to alternative sourcing and the manifestation of Ishmael. But how did he overcome and bounced back? I tell you the truth: because he learned how to factor in thanksgiving in his practice of faith.

A thorough examination of Romans 4:18-21 reveals that Abraham, by giving glory to God, achieved the following:

1. Overcame hopelessness.

2. Strengthened his belief (faith).

3. Overcame weak faith that was precipitated by elongated period of time.

4. Conquered the power of the sense knowledge of his and Sarah's physical condition.

5. Invoked the power of persuasion.

6. Became the father of many nations, thereby validating the truth as it is written in Ecclesiastes 3:14-15 (NIV)...

"I know that everything God does will endure forever; nothing can be added to it and nothing taken from it. God does it so that men will fear him. Whatever is has already been, and what will be has been before; and God will call the past to account."

No doubt faith is a reality and designed by God to provoke the manifestation of the products of His abundant grace. However, the supernatural and realistic nature of faith attracts tremendous obstacles, barriers and hindrances.

Nevertheless, no matter the magnitude and the intensity of the enemies of faith; their overwhelming and physical circumstantial evidences can be terminated by relentless thanksgiving and praise. For sure, the productivity of thanksgiving as a pillar of faith is easily activated by the maintenance of an attitude of praise and thanksgiving as a lifestyle.

Please meditate on the following scriptures until your faith realm is saturated with supernatural springs of thanksgiving. Then begin to function in the realm of adamant faith that Jesus will acknowledge when He comes back (Luke 18:8).

"Always giving thanks to God the Father for everything, in the name of our Lord Jesus Christ." (Ephesians 5:20 NIV)

"Rejoice always, pray continually, give thanks in all circumstances; for this is God's will for you in Christ Jesus." (1 Thessalonians 5:16-18 NIV)

"Now the God of hope fill you with all joy and peace in believing (faith), that ye may abound in hope, through the power of the Holy Ghost." (Romans 15:13 KJV).

This scripture explains that a combination of joy, peace and faith (all of which are supernatural in nature), provokes a divine intervention of the Holy Spirit; who in turn activates the manifestation of our hopeful expectation. Wow! Glory to God. What a powerful revelation.

"Be careful for nothing; but in every thing by prayer and supplication with thanksgiving let your requests be made known unto God.

And the peace of God, which passeth all understanding, shall keep your hearts and minds through Christ Jesus." (Philippians 4:6-7 KJV)

Thanksgiving is the spiritual antidote to doubt, unbelief, worry, anxiety, senses, unstable hearts and minds; all of which are enemies of faith and producers of unanswered prayers.

CHAPTER 25
GRACE - THE SUPER PILLAR
OF FAITH

Without the grace of God there will be no faith of God available to all. A lot has been said about Grace in this book. However, since Grace is inexhaustible, we will continue the exploit. Take a look at Romans 4:16 (KJV).

"Therefore it is of faith, that it might be by grace; to the end the promise might be sure to all the seed; not for that only which is of the law, but to that also which is of faith of Abraham; who is the father of us all."

Let us perform supernatural anatomy of this passage of scripture as follows:

1. Abraham is the father of us all (both Jewish and Gentile believers; Galatians 3:28-29).
2. The seed of Abraham (the seed of Abraham is Christ) is divided into two: those who are of the law (the Jewish believers) and those who are of the faith of Abraham (the Gentile believers).

3. The promise God made to Abraham in Romans 4:13 is that he (Abraham) would be the heir of the world. In other words, God willed the whole world to Abraham.
4. The beneficiary of Abraham's ownership of the whole world is his seed, (Jesus) which comprises both the Jewish and Gentile believers. This is explained in Galatians 3:28-29.
5. God by "grace" (unmerited, unearned, undeserved promises of God), freely gave Abraham the whole world.
6. Because God gave Abraham ownership of the whole world by grace (freely independent of works), God required Abraham and his children to take possession of this gift by faith.

Accordingly, grace begets faith, and faith is the offspring of grace. Both grace and faith cannot be separated. Grace is commonly defined as the unmerited favor of God.

I hereby easily and simply define grace as the portfolio or container housing or holding all the promises and blessings God has freely given to humanity. Also, grace is a free package of the blessings of God, freely delivered to the children of God; following the redemptive works of Jesus Christ. The following scripture can be very helpful: "*And God is able to make all grace abound toward you; that ye, always having all sufficiency in all things, may abound to every good work.*" (11 Corinthians 9:8 KJV)

"*For ye know the grace of our Lord Jesus Christ, that, though he was rich, yet for your sakes he became poor, that ye through his poverty might be rich.*" (11 Corinthians 8:9 KJV)

"And he said unto me, My grace is sufficient for thee: for my strength is made perfect in weakness. Most gladly therefore will I rather glory in my infirmities, that the power of Christ may rest upon me." (11 Corinthians 12:9 KJV)

"For if by one man's offence death reigned by one; much more they which receive abundance of grace and of the gift of righteousness shall reign in life by one, Jesus Christ." (Romans 5:17 KJV)

The phrases: *"all grace abound," "the grace of our Lord Jesus Christ," "my grace is sufficient,"* and *"abundance of grace"* in all the scriptures above reveal the inexhaustibility of the grace of God towards his children.

The vastness and immensity of the grace of God freely delivered to the new creation (believers in Christ) cannot be quantified. But there is a supernatural and outstanding connection between the grace of God and the faith of God.

As stated earlier, without the grace of God, there will be no need for human dimension of the faith of God. A simple explanation is this: Because of the free nature of the grace of God, God requires that the contents of grace must be appropriated by faith.

Without the grace of God there will be no faith of God available to His offspring (believers in Christ).

In another parlance, faith becomes the tool or key with which we take hold of the contents (blessings and promises of God) of the grace of God; freely (independent of efforts or work). The above statement is conspicuously explained by the following scriptures:

"For by grace are ye saved through faith; and that not of yourselves: it is the gift of God: Not of works, lest any man should boast." (Ephesians 2:8-9 KJV)

"Therefore being justified by faith, we have peace with God through our Lord Jesus Christ: By whom also we have access by faith into this grace wherein we stand, and rejoice in hope of the glory of God." (Romans 5:1-2 KJV)

Wow! Access into the grace of God is supernaturally granted by faith. In other words, a practical combination of grace and faith provokes or precipitates the manifestation of our blessings.

Andrew Wommack once said, "Putting faith in God's grace is the path to life."

Again without grace, faith will be irrelevant. And without faith, the grace of God cannot be exploited. Grace therefore is the foundational pillar of faith. This spiritual mindset breaks the power of doubt and unbelief in the sense that what you are hunting by faith; supernaturally exists in the warehouse of grace, which is already your portion. With this mindset, there is no room for doubt.

What are you waiting for? Gone is the era of unanswered biblical prayers and faithless mentality. Now by faith, take hold of what has been freely given to you by grace (Romans 8:32; 1 Corinthians 2:12; 1 Corinthians 3:21-23).

"For all things are for your sakes, that the abundant grace might through the thanksgiving of many redound (abound) to the glory of God."

(11 Corinthians 4:15 KJV).

Brethren, all things are for your sakes through the abundant Grace of God. Do you believe that? Then take a corresponding action of faith.

In conclusion, please, always remember to factor in the element of balance as you deal with grace and faith. In other words, don't ignore the application of faith simply because God has freely granted you His blessings by grace. Also, while releasing your faith, remember that your invisible expectation exists as a supernatural reality in God's warehouse of grace. This grace-faith mindset terminates the monstrous elements of doubt and unbelief.

"For surely there is an end; and thine expectation shall not be cut off." (Proverbs 23:18 KJV)

The foundation of the above promise from God is the abundance of the grace of God for His children (believers in Christ). Also, the gift of abundance of grace and righteousness empower us to exercise ruler-ship and dominion on the Planet Earth.

Grace-faith mindset terminates the monstrous elements of doubt and unbelief.

"For if by one man's offence death reigned by one; much more they which receive abundance of grace and of the gift of righteousness shall reign in life by one, Jesus Christ." (Romans 5:17 KJV).

The above mandate can easily be executed by enforcing a balance of grace and faith. Both grace and faith are two formidable spiritual potent forces we all need to explore to be victorious in our walk with God.

See you at the top, God bless you.

LET US KNOW...

If this book has enriched your life, please, visit us at: www.newcreationfreedomfellowship.org or call: **214-938-5368**, and be a part of what the Lord is doing through this ministry.